FIRE FROM THE ASHES

Reflections on Lighting the Shadows

edited by Kim Uyede-Kai

To Pattie -
Fuel for the
fire on your journey.
Blessings.
Kim

Fire from the Ashes: Reflections on Lighting the Shadows

11/95 3.5M

ISBN # 0-88622-338-5

The United Church of Canada
3250 Bloor Street West
Etobicoke, ON M8X 2Y4

Editor: Kim Uyede-Kai
Cover Design: Gordon Szendrey
Book Design: Dept. of Graphics and Print Production
Printed in Canada

Contents

Acknowledgements

All biblical quotations are from the *New Revised Standard Version*.

Micklem, Caryl ed. *More Contemporary Prayers: Prayers on Fifty-two Themes.* (London: SCM Press Ltd.) 1970.

Ellison, Ralph *Invisible Man.* (New York: The Modern Library) 1992.

Kawano, Roland *The Global City.* (Winfield: Wood Lake Books, Inc.) 1992.

Hill, Daniel G. *The Freedom Seekers: Blacks in Early Canada.* (Agincourt: The Book Society of Canada) 1981, 26.

Akers, Doris Copyright 1958 by MANNA MUSIC, 2111 Kenmere Ave., Burbank, CA 91504 USA. Copyright secured. All Rights Reserved.

Heyward, Carter "Living for the Living: Theological Lessons from Nicaragua," Davis, Ellen C., ed. *Speaking of Christ: A Lesbian Feminist Voice.* (New York: The Pilgrim Press) 1989.

hooks, bell *Outlaw Culture: Resisting Representation.* (New York: Routledge) 1994.

Park, Andrew Sung *The Wounded Heart of God: The Asian Concept of Han and the Christian Doctrine of Sin.* (Nashville: Abingdon Press) 1993.

Volavkova, Hana, ed. *...I Never Saw Another Butterfly...: Children's Drawings and Poems from Terezin Concentration Camp 1942-1944.* (New York: Schocken Books) 1993.

Maria del Nevo *The New Internationalist*, #240. February 1993, 22.

Oates, Stephen B. *Let the Trumpet Sound: The Life of Martin Luther King, Jr.* (New York: New American Library) 1982.

Bennett, Lerone Jr. *What Manner of Man: A Biography of Martin Luther King, Jr. 1929-1968.* (Chicago: Johnson Publishing Company Inc.) 1976.

Mary Crow Dog *Lakota Woman.* (Grove Weidenfeld) 1990.

Foreword

Thanks and appreciation go to many people who saw this book come about:

to Wayne Irwin, Division of Mission in Canada, Worship Contract Staff, who brought calm and peace to many missed deadlines and who coordinated the production so capably;

to E. Leicester Bigby and members of the former Ethnic Ministries Working Unit, who initiated the idea of a lenten reflections book with racial minority voices and who persisted in seeing their vision materialize;

to Flora Litt and Roland Kawano whose insightful comments on the initial manuscript were extremely helpful;

to Christopher Dumas, Division of Communication, and Gordon Szendrey, cover designer, for their creative skills;

to Mary Rose Donnelly, Division of Mission in Canada Resource Production, and Kathryn Lingwood, copy editor, for getting the right words in print;

to Fred Graham, Division of Mission in Canada, Worship, who began the process;

to my sons, Trevor and Jeremy, for providing loving support and many a distraction to ensure that this project did not consume my life;

to Brian for converting faxes to readable disk format, emergency copy typing, and knowing when to take the boys out of the house.

Introduction

Ashes. The beginning of Lent. Christ's walk to suffering, rejection; in companionship, then ultimately alone. Who can better identify with that lonely walk than those who have been there?

With humility, vulnerability, and candour, seven writers share their reflections as people of colour who have lived long in the shadows of the church. They speak from their diverse and often painful experiences of racism, rejection, and their search for belonging and acceptance in God's world. Shadows are not always dwelling places for that which is bad, evil or unknown. Like a fearful child who imagines all his or her room's dark shadows to be monsters until a light switched on reveals harmless, ordinary things, their stories begin to cast light on that which appears to the unseeing as dark and colourless.

For most racial minorities, there are few opportunities or encouragement to reflect theologically as people of colour among accepting, safe communities. For most of the writers, this was their first invitation to write from the whole of their experiences. It was not always easy. Challenged to read the scriptures and walk with Jesus in new ways, the process was a lenten journey in itself, from personal wilderness to communal resurrection.

While each writer comes from very diverse heritage and church experiences, the stories they share are an accessible invitation to all readers to engage in their own reflections and to meditate on their own life stories, privately or in community. Just as ashes, the lifeless residue of spent energy, can bring forth new growth and new life from the earth, the journeys of the writers have led to life-giving experiences with the One who identifies with the outcast, the refugee, the other—the ministering, suffering, and risen Christ.

Put on the lenten ashes of the writers' experiences and live the fiery passions of their journeys to Easter. In doing so, you might discover your own ashes leading you to your own life-giving fire in the way of Jesus.

Kim Uyede-Kai

Part One - Cry Unto God

Ash Wednesday

FIRE AND ASHES

Marilou Carrillo

AMOS 5: 6-15
"Seek the Lord and live."

When I was in a Guatemalan refugee camp in Campeche, Mexico, Francisca and her 14-year old daughter Martina cooked corn tortillas and boiled beans or hierbas (herbs) over an open fire. They gathered the wood from a few kilometres away and carried it on their heads or on a bike over parched limestone trails in the blazing heat of the Yucatan.

As I watched them and the fire, as I smelled the smoke, I was enveloped by a warmth in the very cave of my heart. Here was fire breathing life into the corn of the earth harvested by their own hands—or by the hands of others when they bought corn in big sacks because the previous season's drought did not yield their share of harvest. Here were fire and ashes as living testament to the Mayans who fled from their villages in 1982 when the military burned their homes to the ground in a scorched earth policy to eliminate the Mayans from their land. Here was fire as witness to their desperate, terrifying race to escape death, seek life, and survive.

REFLECTION RITUAL
Watch a log burn or paper burning in a suitable container.

Meditate on human and divine paradox: fire as evil energy that can lead to death, fire as divine energy of destruction, heat as warmth for transformation, ashes as debris of these energies, light that sparks clearer vision.

Meditate on the connection between the words of the peasant farmer of Tekoa hills in Judah in the 8th century B.C.E.—that Yahweh will burn the cities of those who strangle the poor—and the stories of Guatemalan Mayans today—evil and injustice tried to overtake their lives and souls as they fled their burning homes.

Meditate on God as raging fire and God as heat and light.

What do you need to offer to the transforming fire of God?

PRAYER

O Source of all fire,
Fire of destruction and of
    transformation,
Fire yielding light, heat, and
    ashes,
This cycle of fire and ashes from
    destruction
and death to nourishment and
    life
is hard to bear.

Grant to those who are poor
in our streets and
neighbourhoods today
Your justice
to place their sticks
and firewood into your hearth
To transform their world of fire
and ashes,
of loss and want,
and ours of gain and affluence,
To a world of living firewood.
Nourish all who stoke the fire.
O Source of all fire,
Fire of destruction and of
transformation,
Fire yielding light, heat, and
ashes,
Stand with us that we may bear
this cycle of fire and ashes
so all may live in your warmth
and your light.

Thursday

The Power of Prayer

Karyn Bigby

Habbakuk 3:1-10

"O Lord, I have heard of your renown, and I stand in awe, O Lord, of your work. In our own time revive it; in our own time make it known; in wrath may you remember mercy."

Like Habbakuk, many times we question what is happening in the world around us. Why is there war in Bosnia? Why did an earthquake devastate Kobe, Japan? Why did millions have to suffer and die in Rwanda and Burundi? Why the political unrest and struggle in Haiti? Why is there AIDS and other incurable diseases?

Habbakuk wrote his prayer in a time of impending disaster. In his struggle against adversity, he shows us that we can get through difficulties by trusting God, for God will never forsake us. As Joel exhorts us, we must "...cry unto the Lord" (Joel 1:14) when we are in trouble. However, we should not wait until things get bad to pray. Paul exhorts us in Ephesians 6:18 and 1 Thessalonians 5:17 that we should pray at all times.

Prayer can be so powerful that God answers before we have finished praying. While Daniel was still praying, the angel Gabriel flew to him with the answer. (Daniel 9:20-23) Isaiah tells us that "Before they call I will answer, while they are yet speaking, I will hear." (Isaiah 65:24)

God does not grant our every request. Sometimes our requests conflict with God's highest good for us: "For my thoughts are not your thoughts, neither are your ways my ways saith the Lord." (Isaiah 55:8) Though we do not understand the suffering going on around us, God has a plan. We must have faith like Habbakuk that God's will and intention toward us is always loving.

A woman with whom I sing in a gospel choir in my church is recovering from a major illness which required surgery. Before her operation, just as she was surrendering to the anaesthesia, all she could think of were the words of a Lionel Ritchie song. It was a prayer for God to help the children and not let them fall by the side of the road. This became her prayer. Although she is still undergoing treatment, she is here today worshipping and singing. This song has a whole new meaning for her and the other members of the choir because it helped to sustain her in her time of suffering. This was a powerful prayer indeed.

REFLECTION

What incident in your life, or the life of someone you know, has been a struggle with adversity?

How has prayer changed your life or theirs?

PRAYER

God, as we look upon the world
and see the evil and
suffering in it,
we easily doubt your goodness
and your purpose.
Help us beyond our doubts to
faith.
There is much of which we
cannot be certain,
and yet in Jesus we see enough
to know that you love us.
Help us and all people to accept
your purpose.
And, as we consider Jesus, to see
by faith that nothing
—no suffering, no evil—
can finally frustrate your will.[1]

Friday

A FAMILY OF RICHES

Nena Cervantes

PHILIPPIANS 4:10-20
"And my God will fully satisfy every need of yours according to God's riches in glory in Christ Jesus."

When I was seven-years old, my parents flew from the Philippines to the United States for what the entire family thought would be a brief business assignment for my father. They left behind a very young brood of seven daughters and three sons (one more daughter was on a scholarship in the U.S. and eagerly anticipated a reunion with them).

I distinctly remember the air of sadness as my brothers, sisters, and I watched them board the plane. One brother, then 11-years old, was crying, but I cannot recall myself weeping, perhaps knowing intuitively that my feelings lay too deep for tears.

Now that I am grown, there have been many private moments when, through the full wisdom of hindsight, I realize how sad the scene was for the whole family. At first, the intent was for father to stay for a few months, but as those months tallied up to 12, then two years and more, my parents saw fit to send for us all, one by one. U.S. Immigration thought otherwise.

In the process of trying to obtain a visa to the United States, I would go during class hours to the U.S. embassy, a gleaming white building on Manila Bay surrounded by iron gates. By age nine, the possibility of joining my parents seemed imminent, and so my schooling stopped before I could complete grade four. A delegation of teachers dropped by our home to bid me farewell toting Philippine handicrafts as presents. On my last day in school, my classmates, though excited at the prospect of me playing in snow, wept at the thought of losing me. That night, I packed presents into one suitcase only to unpack them because the visa was once again denied. I repeated grade four, but by mid-year had done well enough to rejoin former classmates already in grade five.

I did not join my parents until a few weeks short of my eleventh birthday. Half my childhood had gone by without them. My brothers and sisters had been transformed into adolescents and young adults as veritable orphans. My brother, who had wept so profusely when he was eleven, would not see my parents again until he was 18.

Though our nuclear family was "orphaned" for seven years, our extended family of cousins, uncles, and aunts, and our community—including our community of faith—provided the support so direly needed. The family is a vibrant part of Philippine society, and its vibrancy was most felt during the physical absence of our parents. At the U.S. embassy, the consul responded to my family as another file in their bulging cabinet of immigration cases, but our neighbours responded to us as family. God supplied our familial needs through nurturing neighbours, concerned teachers, caring congregants, and loving relatives.

REFLECTION

Who is family to you?

How can we appreciate God's riches during times when we feel needy?

PRAYER

Nurturing God,
May we see Your world
through childlike eyes again,
appreciating with wide-eyed
wonder
the riches You supply.

Saturday

THAT ALL MAY BE ONE?

Richard Chung-sik Choe

JOHN 17:9-19

"(God), protect them in your name that you have given me, so that they may be one, as we are one."

"I am an invisible man....I am a man of substance, of flesh and bone, fiber and liquids—and I might even be said to possess a mind. I am invisible, simply because people refuse to see me."[2] Thus begins Ralph Ellison's *Invisible Man*. It is about being Black in the United States in the '50s.

Ellison's opening lines came to me while I was attending a conference a few years ago. The theme was "That All May Be One"—the spirit of our church as a "united" and a "uniting" church. Yet, throughout the conference, I began to wonder about the meaning of being one. Each time I saw the leaders and facilitators I realized how "white" our church was, a painful reminder that I was a minority. Majorities do not often notice exclusion, since they see images of themselves all around them. However, minorities like myself notice exclusion when we are not present in the leadership.

One day, my four-year old daughter, Frances, was drawing pictures of the world around her, expressing her wonderment and joy of life. As she was proudly showing me her art work, my heart began to sink. No matter how hard I looked I could not find her in the pictures. I asked her where she was. "Daddy! Here! This is me. Can't you see?" It was a dancing, smiling, happy girl with blond hair and very pale skin. I was heartbroken that my dark-haired child had drawn pictures where her authentic image was nowhere to be seen. She had learned in her short life that being "white" is best, and that to be otherwise is to be invisible.

Frances's process of liberation began right away. Sung, my wife, and I explained to her about the black hair we have and how beautiful it is, about the different skin colours people have, and that she should be proud to be Korean Canadian.

Like my daughter's pictures, I cannot see myself in the structure of the church. It is like looking into an empty mirror and searching for an image of myself that is not there. The church is far from being one. Being one is to be in mutual relationship and mutual acceptance—to be welcoming and to be welcomed, not just being included as the other. It is, as Roland Kawano says, "valuing everyone alike, not making everyone alike."[3]

I have an image of an ever-widening circle. Through this process we all include one another. I dream of the day when the *whole* people of God will genuinely be *whole*.

REFLECTION

Have there ever been times when you felt "invisible"?

What are ways in which we can include one another in each other's space/community, where everyone can feel an integral part of the whole?

PRAYER

God of unity,
we pray for your guidance as
we seek to be One with our
brothers and sisters.
We ask that you show us ways
in which we can invite one
another
to be companions on the way to
Wholeness.
When we become weary of too
many differences among us,
when we get nervous about
trying each other's ways
and when we have difficulty
valuing one another's gifts,
remind us of your call for us to
be One.

Part Two - Follow Me

1st Sunday in Lent

A FAITH FOR SURVIVAL

Eleanor Scarlett

DANIEL 9:3-10

"Then I turned to the Lord God, to seek an answer by prayer and supplication with fasting and sackcloth and ashes."

The book of Daniel was written during a time of great suffering of the Jews. They were removed from their country, religion, and culture. They endured great persecution, oppression, exploitation, and isolation. This particular passage invites us to walk with those who suffered.

I am a descendant of enslaved Africans. My people and I have been oppressed for many years. We were taken against our will from our countries, leaving behind our homes, families, friends, religions, and cultures. We suffered greatly at the hands of our captors. We were whipped, prevented from practising our religious rites, not even allowed to pray to our gods. We could not speak in our own languages. All that we once knew was taken from us. We endured and we survived.

While growing up in Jamaica, I lived among a harmonious people, very diverse in cultural, racial, and religious backgrounds. Though economically poor, they were rich in their faith and beliefs, believing that God would deliver them from their poverty and sustain them in their fight to achieve economic equality. The depth of their faith was overwhelming. They were able to see God through their suffering. They firmly believed that the God who delivered Daniel would also deliver them. And that wherever God dwells, peace, love, and justice abides.

Upon immigrating to Canada, I found myself removed from the extended family support and faith community that I grew up with. I felt isolated in a culture other than my own. I longed for the "innocent" faith that was handed down to me. Although Canada has been my home for many years, I still crave the spirituality I knew of former times.

I have often reflected on the faith of my ancestors and realized that without their faith, they would never have endured such suffering. My grandmothers referred to Christ as the Suffering Saviour, the One who would liberate them from their struggles, the One who walked and talked with them. They took their struggles to God who redeems and sanctifies, and often said that "only Christ understands us completely." This is the type of faith that nurtured me and continues to help me through my own difficulties and my experiences of the societal forces of evil that create racism, sexism, classism, and economic oppression. Nurturing our faith in Christ is the only answer to eliminating these evil forces that oppress us.

REFLECTION

When have you longed for the spirituality of the past?

Whose faith in the face of suffering has nurtured you?

PRAYER

Imagine Christ beside you. Talk to God in your own words, your own language. Talk about your own struggles, that which oppresses you, that which gives you strength. Ask for whatever you need to meet those struggles with faith.

Monday

SHARED FLESH AND BLOOD

Alex Kasirye-Musoke

HEBREWS 2:10-18

"Since, therefore, the children share flesh and blood, he himself likewise shared the same things...."

Among us are people who are experiencing untold suffering under oppression and male-fashioned and male-dominated political, economic, and social systems. Beaten, raped, abused, and exploited, suffering is their daily experience. Many are now refugees scattered all over the world; 80 per cent are women and children. Forced out of their homelands by government sponsored violence, many now live in our midst, but most of us try not to get involved with them. Sometimes we look down on them as intruders, as people who have not been educated as we have, who do not speak our language, and who do not integrate into our way of doing things. Sometimes we close our doors to them, and shut our eyes and ears because we do not wish to see their tears or hear them cry. Perhaps we are afraid to know why they are displaced and why they suffer.

In keeping them apart from us, we often forget that they are people of the same flesh and blood. We forget that

Jesus was a refugee when his parents ran away with him to Egypt to escape from Herod's violence. I can identify with this suffering servant who had to flee for his life for I, too, am a refugee who experienced displacement and homelessness and the utter loss of my home and my life in Uganda. Shared experiences, shared flesh and blood.

The book of Hebrews is explicit in spelling out Jesus' humanity, rejection, suffering, and endurance of death. He became human, suffered, and died in order to destroy death, to set everyone free, and open up channels of communication between all people. Therefore, human nature is important in the process of redemption, for it determined the form in which Jesus had to come. He had to become the same flesh and blood to redeem us and make us one with God.

We are the people who have come from all over. Despite our differences, we all share a common humanity, just as Jesus shared our same humanity, and became like his sisters and brothers. Let us gather at our common life-giving source, Jesus the Christ.

Reflection

Recollect a time when you had to flee, if not your home, then perhaps a personal or work-related situation, a relationship.

How does that experience connect you with Jesus, the refugee? with countless other displaced persons?

Prayer

Loving God,
You have gathered all the nations together
and made us into your worldwide family.
Help us to be loyal to one another
and to serve all people selflessly.
Let your spirit inspire us continually.
In Jesus' name we pray.

Tuesday

FOLLOW THE LEADER

Kim Uyede-Kai

MARK 1:14-28
"And Jesus said to them, 'Follow me....'"

Shuffle cross front, leap, pick-up toe, ball change. My fumbling tap shoe clad feet struggled to get all the right steps and still make contact with the floor. As an adult, I take tap classes, having wanted lessons as a child but not having had the time or money.

I was a beginner, mistakenly enrolled in an intermediate class; so I had to learn very quickly. The hardest part was remembering the order the steps came in. The will to learn came from childhood, but my brain's retentive capacity had aged.

Fortunately, with each new step, my instructor made sure she was always in front by running around us whenever we changed directions. Once we caught on, she was able to teach from one place. When she stepped back and we danced on our own, she continued to call out the steps until eventually we were able to do a whole routine alone. Even when we performed on stage, she still prompted from the wings.

Learning dance routines is somewhat like the children's game of Follow the Leader. The leader moves and the followers copy the movement. Followers don't know what the leader will do next, but if they are attentive, they eventually catch on. Those near the end of the line sometimes can't see the leader, so they follow those who can. Then the leadership changes.

Within the church we now talk about leadership that empowers others, leadership that models a different kind of power from the autocratic, authoritative leader of the past. To lead today is to be both leader and follower, taking cues from the followers and slowing down when followers are having trouble keeping up, and speeding things up when they are able to move on to more difficult things.

Jesus said, "Follow me." Unlike a military command, following Jesus is not about mindlessly doing what one is told. Inherent in Jesus' command is the understanding that he leads, in some ways, like a dance teacher. He dances along with us, sometimes in front, sometimes beside, sometimes behind, patiently re-teaching what some forget, gradually pulling back, but still leading from the wings.

Jesus says, "Follow me."
Dare we dance in the following?
Dare we follow in the dancing?

Reflection

As you are able, play a simple game of Follow the Leader with a small group. One person as the Leader moves around a circle any way s/he wishes for about a minute, changing the movements periodically with the rest copying. Keep the movements simple and the rhythm constant. Then pass the leadership over to the next person in the circle. Keep changing leadership around the circle until everyone has led and followed.

When have you experienced/ needed a leader who could lead from all sides as well as be a follower?

How do you experience Christ leading you in the dance in your life?

Prayer

Dancing, Leader God,
Alive in the movements of our
feet
and in our hearts;
Patiently guiding us when we
stumble;
Never judging whether our
rhythms
are in sync with the song
by the world's standards.
Spirit of Boundless Energy,
always near,
lead us in the living dance,
to follow faithfully, responsively,
passionately.

Wednesday

When the Heart and the Womb are One

Marilou Carrillo

Mark 1: 29-45

"Then the fever left her, and she began to serve them."

My eyes were half-opened. I watched him come closer to the foot of my bed. The women were rushing about, glancing at him, staring at me, and mumbling noisily. The men were standing outside by the door, mute, peering in and posturing to do "something." I strained to see my daughter behind her husband, who was behind the Teacher. I was agitated by having a man, a stranger, in my home and by my bed. I opened my eyes and greeted him. He returned my salutation.

I was shivering and my body ached down to the marrow. He said something, and I cringed in pain. I shut my eyes tightly and waited for the wave of agony rising from my womb to pass. What demon is this that has punished me so? Is there no relief from suffering? Ever since I gave birth to her my body has been beaten down by childbirth, by work: fetching water, cooking by the fire, washing clothes, cleaning the house, being with the women in their grief, with children dying from mysterious diseases. I am tired. Death is the silence that will free my body at last. Will I survive this day?

I shook in disbelief. I opened my eyes. The Teacher took my right hand, put his arm around my neck, and lifted me up. This proximity to the warmth of a stranger was unbearable. I wept silently, tears flowing onto his chest. Only I could hear the deep sobbing from times past. The pain and tears of my mother, her mother, the mothers before them. Only then did I realize how alone I had been. To be a woman had always meant people and family surrounded me. I served all of them for so long. My illness suddenly became clear to me. It was the alienation of the heart. When did it all begin? Was it my heart, or my womb, that stopped beating? My life blood had left...when? Now I was one with this stranger, and with all of them in this room, out there on the street, my ancestors. The blood from my womb and my heart is flowing again!

I will be healed. My life will continue, to minister, yes, but from a throbbing womb and a beating heart. I bid death farewell while I choose to live, until the cycle of life begins at the end of mine.

REFLECTION RITUAL

Find a picture, letter, or object of a woman who has struggled, been ill, or has died. Place this in front of you as you sit in a quiet place. Play music she might like or light a candle.

What is the woman you have chosen saying to you about the presence or absence of healing, creativity, service, and ministering in her life?

Reflect on your experiences of alienation and of times when you served but were filled with resentment. Can you truly serve and minister only when you are healed?

Can healing only happen in community, when your heart is one with others?

PRAYER

O You Who Are Our Heart
Lay your hand on my chest.
Surround my heart with sweet
honey
To soften her walls and open up
to you.
Free my heart of loneliness and
alienation.
Blow a warm breeze so I may
begin to sway
Along with the Heartbeat of the
universe
Your very own Body.

O You Who Are Our Womb,
Lay your head on your woman's womb.
Hold your container of seeds and sap
To nestle in among the juices of my life.
Free the womb of fear, guilt, and resentment.
Stir the gentle earth in me that I may begin to grow
Beside the Wombthrob of all creation
Your very own Body.

O You Who Are Our Heart and Womb
Source of all life and creation,
We rise up in health and life
In gratitude and humility, power and conviction.
We know that the blood of life flows
In our hearts and wombs in unity with yours
To co-create a world in need of awakening and healing,
For all who are living and dying for the love of your justice.

Thursday

FAITH IN ACTION

Karyn Bigby

MARK 2:1-12

"...They removed the roof above him; and after having dug through it, they let down the mat on which the paralytic lay."

This story of resourceful friends bringing their helpless friend to Jesus reminds me of the many people who made up the Underground Railroad. This network of slaves, freed slaves, and anti-slavery sympathizers worked to help slaves to freedom by guiding them north to Canada. As described by historian Daniel G. Hill in his book, *The Freedom Seekers: Blacks in Early Canada*, the Underground Railroad consisted of "employees" who were mainly Quakers; "stockholders" who financed the operation; and "conductors" and "stationkeepers" who received, fed, clothed, and hid new arrivals at transfer points.[4]

The very lives of the runaway slaves were at risk. Travelling through swamps and forests at night and without food often proved to be fatal. A caught slave was killed, maimed or badly beaten by his or her slave owner or by the authorities in the South to deter others who may be entertaining the notion of running away to freedom.

Though many in the Underground Railroad chose to challenge these obstacles, one woman in particular exemplifies the type of "faith in action" for which we as Christians strive.

Harriet Tubman, dubbed the "Black Moses" of her people, led her fellow slaves to freedom. After her own escape in 1849 she led about 30 trips north and helped over 1,000 slaves escape. Though illiterate, Harriet Tubman was considered "a military genius, a master of logistics and strategy."[5] Travelling at night, she used the North Star as her compass.

Another tool used by Harriet Tubman and her fellow slaves was the Negro spiritual. These songs were powerful expressions of the intense faith of an oppressed people. Spirituals like "Steal Away," "De Gospel Train" ("Git on Board, Little Children"), "Hush, Hush, Somebody's Callin Mah Name," and many others formed a secret communication amongst the slaves. These songs were used to signal to slaves that the Underground Railroad would be running that night.

As a Black woman today, the obstacles I face are not as overt as those faced by Harriet Tubman and her compatriots. They are covert and include racism, sexism, and prejudice. With God's help, I strive to overcome them by being the best that I can be. Sometimes that's not enough.

I recently walked into a place of business to be told that "the jobs are all filled." I was not there for a job and most certainly, with two university degrees, would be grossly overqualified for the type of job for which it was thought I was applying. The receptionist merely saw me as a skin colour.

The obstacles I face today can be disheartening. However, I find music helps me keep in touch with Jesus. I sing in a gospel choir and find that in glorifying God through song, my own faith is strengthened. Many of the songs my choir sings are the same spirituals the slaves sang to express their faith. The lyrics and the melodies are powerful, and I feel an affinity with these trail blazers, even though my experiences are different and could be deemed trivial by comparison.

Prayer is another important way of overcoming obstacles. I pray to God to enlighten those who judge me by my skin colour or by my sex.

Reflection

What are the obstacles facing you?

How do you express your faith in action? What assists and supports you?

Friday

LIGHT FOR THE JOURNEY

Nena Cervantes

I CORINTHIANS 4: 1-7

"Therefore do not pronounce judgement before the time, before the Lord comes, who will bring to light the things now hidden in darkness and will disclose the purposes of the heart. Then each one will receive commendation from God."

In 1994 I took a "Learning for Leadership" course at the Centre for Christian Studies in Toronto. The class was comprised of a cross-section of active church members interested in honing leadership skills for the benefit of their respective churches. It was an intensive six month programme, the goals of which were practical skills, confidence, and personal growth as a Christian. Most of us began as strangers. Slowly we built a sense of community in the group through weekly rituals and the sharing of symbols.

On the last week, we stayed overnight at the Centre. We supped together, savouring potluck dishes which coordinated so serendipitously. While eating, we summarized how the week had gone for us with touching informality, punctuated by bantering here and there.

PRAYER

Lord, don't move this mountain
but give me strength to climb it.
Please don't move that stumbling block,
but lead me Lord, around it.

The way may not be easy
You didn't say that it would be
For when my tribulations get too light,
I tend to stray from Thee.

Now when my foes would slay me
and these things they will try to do
O, Lord, don't touch them, but within their hearts
make them give their hearts to you.

Our cares we bring unto You
You told us that we could
for you help those who try to help themselves
and I believe we should.

Lord, don't move this mountain
but give me strength to climb it.
Please don't move that stumbling block,
but lead me Lord, around it.[6]

When supper was done, we gathered around a coffee table to share faith journeys. Symbols came to life: jewelry, toys, gifts from the earth and sea, art objects, pictures, even mundane objects took on deep personal meaning. One of our group was missing, yet acknowledged, for our stories went into a tape recorder for her to share later. Our circle was inclusive.

The room was dimly lit when we began, but slowly brightened with every story told. Each time someone finished telling their faith journey, a candle would be lit. The candle lighting ceremony was poignant, akin to lighting Platonic caves once pitch dark. In the darkness we groped and stumbled, but now there was light for future journeys...or was light already there? Was light always present without our knowledge, while we were blinded by our doubt, panic or anxiety? Like matchsticks poised for ignition by friction?

Wicks were lit one by one. Soft brightness bathed the table as a collective baptism of fire immersed the table in a river of light. I felt in my palpitating heart that beyond wax and wick another light held us with palpable warmth. I felt it tremulously and awesomely in my soul as we each held up treasured, inspiring symbols.

As a result of sharing our faith journeys, a collective awakening allowed us to see through a third eye that the light was always present though it flickered in the wind, sometimes snuffed out, but lit anew by a pilot lighting system. That night, the group became a community through our common faith.

Reflection

Where are you lighting a candle in faith?

What symbols do we share with others so that our faith journeys extend from personal to communal?

What experiences are we willing to share to establish a foundation of trust?

Prayer

The moon is full tonight,
bright with borrowed light.
Lend us Your light that we may
see
and fear not.
May we be wicks waiting
to be ignited by Your light.

Saturday

Those Who are in Need

Richard Chung-sik Choe

Mark 2:13-22

"Those who are well have no need of a physician, but those who are sick; I have come to call not the righteous but sinners."

I see more and more people panhandling in downtown cities. Sign of our times. It is very uncomfortable passing by those who look very hungry.

Many people are moving out to the suburbs where the air is cleaner and poverty is usually not seen on the streets. Fewer churches are left in the downtown areas. With the migration of people, churches have also been moving out of the inner city. It is very important to develop new churches for the people where they live. Yet I cannot help asking myself, "At what price are we pouring out so many of our resources into new suburban church development? Are we a church that is budget-driven or mission-driven? Are we abandoning the poor by following money into the suburbs?"

There was a beautiful church being built in the midst of a slum in South Korea. It was to be a symbol of God's blessing for the church members. However, each evening on their way home after long hours of hard labour, some of the neighbours would pass by the construction sight and throw stones at the church, cursing and breaking the beautiful stained glass windows. For the poor, the sight of the cathedral-like church was the sign of sheer stupidity and oppression—religion gone wrong. How could anybody spend such an enormous amount of money on a church building when all around were signs of poverty? Why couldn't these Christians use the money for the poor in their neighbourhood?

When I see beautifully decorated churches I cannot help asking the same question the poor neighbours in South Korea asked. How do we justify the financing of building such ornate churches when we are cutting money to the mission and outreach parts of our church? Is financial difficulty an excuse for being the "church for the self" rather than "church for the other"? Do churches need hotel-like interiors?

The time of Reformation was marked by the simplicity and stripping of church interiors. They believed that the ornaments in the sanctuary would hinder their focus on the Word, the Bible. *Sola Scriptura*—cleaning the temple of unnecessary gizmos. I wonder whether the time has come for us to do the same.

How can we say we love God whom we have not seen and be apathetic to the poor and marginalized brothers and sisters we can see? This is what I hear from Jesus in today's passage. Jesus calls us to discover the interconnectedness of life. Life together in Christ means life together in community, struggling to welcome and include all. Carter Heyward says that "our responsibility is to live as interdependent members of a Body-which is to be human, fully human."[7] To be fully human is to be fully connected with all the members of human community. Poverty dehumanizes us all — the rich and the poor—because to be human is to be in a just relationship with one another and with God. When that relationship is broken, we all are de-humanized.

Reflection

We as the church have a history of being for and with the needy and the marginalized. How do we continue to be faithful to that commitment?

How much of our personal budget do we spend on the needy? How much of our local congregation's budget goes for mission?

Prayer

God of the Poor,
help us to meet you where you call us,
not where we want you to be.
We confess that it is much easier to focus
on what we need for ourselves and the people around us.
It is too much for us to see
those who are in need of our support.
Help us to realize that each one of us on this planet
is connected and that when one suffers
we all suffer in some way.
We pray that you encourage us
to find you in those we meet in our lives.

Part Three - A Way Out of No Way

2nd Sunday in Lent

THE IMPOSSIBLE IS POSSIBLE

Eleanor Scarlett

GENESIS 41:14-45
"Then Pharaoh sent for Joseph, and he was hurriedly brought out of the dungeon."

I am Atoma, the second youngest in my family. One day I went with my friends to gather firewood. We met some men who showed us some fancy things. I felt uncomfortable and afraid. Remembering what we were told by the elders about strangers, I signalled to my friends and we began to run. I fell and the men caught up with me and locked me in a room. I was never so frightened in my life as I was that day. It was days before they took me to a ship waiting at the wharf. I was placed in chains and taken to the bottom of the ship. There I realized there were many others from my country on the ship. I was not alone.

I began to sing and pray to the God of my parents and this helped my days become shorter. The singing and praying also helped my sanity. I felt that despite my situation, I was in God's hands and would be helped. I often had dreams that things would happen and that somehow God would use me to make a difference.

One night, there was a raging storm at sea. Everyone was terrified, including the captain. I was not afraid in the least because I felt God's presence with me. I knew that deep within my heart, the God of love would keep me during these frightening moments. Someone told me that the captain had summoned me. I was shaking like a leaf and wondered what I had done to deserve this, but deep down I still felt that God would protect me. The captain wanted to know why, despite the storm, I was so very calm. So I told him about my God.

I prayed right there in front of the captain and the storm ceased. He and the rest of the crew were amazed at what they thought was my power. I explained to them that I had no power on my own. It was the Creator of all peoples that calmed the storm. The captain was moved with compassion and gave me my freedom.

God's love prevails even in the darkest hours and corners of our lives. God can make a way out of no way. God's love was made evident when Jesus the Christ brought about liberation to all people. It is this God that we serve who is able to turn the impossible into the possible.

Reflection
When in your experience has God made a way for you when there seemed none?

Prayer

God of love, peace, and justice,
we ask that you reveal yourself
to us anew.
Enter our hearts and lives, and
bring joy to the broken-
hearted.
May your love flow down like a
river into our lives,
so that your children everywhere
may find a new understanding in
you.

Monday

Called to Set Aside

Alex Kasirye-Musoke

Mark 3:7-19a
"...They came to him in great numbers from Judea, Jerusalem, Idumea, beyond the Jordan, and the region around Tyre and Sidon."

Mark puts Jesus right in the middle of a circle, the centre of attraction. Men, women, children, the sick, the hungry, the lame, the poor, the blind came from all directions to meet Jesus or have a glimpse of him. Everyone in the region put everything aside and came. Reports of his deeds, his kind words, his blessings, and the help rendered to all who came had spread to all corners. He healed the sick. He healed broken relationships. He fed the hungry.

Surely Jesus never sent a message out to invite people to come. People heard what he did and they came. His deeds were persuasive enough to invite people to him. Jesus touched, changed, and empowered many lives. The changed lives of those who came into contact with Christ exhibited his goodness and invited others to come for the same experience. For many, joy displaced bitterness and fear. His love cast out fear.

Before I entered ordered ministry

I was a teacher and consultant of economics in Uganda. Money was plentiful and life was quite comfortable. It gradually became clear to me that I had to set aside the wealth and pomp of my chosen field if I were to serve God and not just myself. However, there was much I had to put aside in order to come to Jesus. It was not easy to leave behind financial security, privilege, and the desire to always strive for the top. Nor was it easy to see many of my Ugandan friends in my former field of economics subsequently get into deep, political trouble, some of whom were killed. It could easily have happened to me. In coming to Jesus, I had put aside things I did not know I was setting aside.

The Jesus who attracted great multitudes is the same Jesus we believe in today. He is always inviting us to himself by word of his deeds. We continue to put everything aside to come to him.

REFLECTION

What are you being called to set aside to come to meet Jesus?

How are you being changed by your encounter?

PRAYER

Almighty God,
you are a God of all colours.
Thank you that you created us
male and female.
Thank you for our human
nature.
Help us to celebrate and to see
in all human relationships
the cross of Christ as the only
way to peace.
Set us free from blindness that
we may see you
in all your creation.

Tuesday

ON THE WAY TO THE COMICS

Kim Uyede-Kai

MARK 3:19B-35

"If a kingdom is divided against itself, that kingdom cannot stand. And if a house is divided against itself, that house will not be able to stand."

Several days of newspapers often stack up before I get through them. But reading the newspaper is a must for me. I need to see in print what is going on in the world beyond me and what other people are thinking.

I know people who no longer read newspapers because hearing about so many problems in the world adds too much stress to their already over-stressed lives. If only they could buy a paper with just good news, like sports, entertainment, and human interest stories. And comics.

There are days when I scan the papers and only see the funny or quirky news while on my way to the comics page. I have been called up on some of these occasions by my son who is horrified to see me lingering over a picture of mutilated people when in fact I am reading an article on cow dung lower down. I hadn't even seen the picture that disturbed him so much. And that disturbs me.

At times the newspaper is too painful or disturbing to read. Into the newspaper basket it goes, guaranteed to resurface sooner or later when I have the time and the emotional space to read it. Such an article was the story about Korean "comfort women," kidnapped and enslaved in prostitution during Japan's brutal occupation of the Korean Peninsula and other parts of Asia.

Even though I am of Japanese ancestry, I did not identify with the Japanese military men nor feel shame that "my people" committed such atrocities. "My people" are Canadians of Japanese descent who were enslaved in Canadian internment camps during the Second World War, not those with whom I share genetic origins in Japan. The Asian women victims were also "my people"—women. Women who bore horrors too excruciating to hear: kidnapped, raped repeatedly by Japanese officers and lesser ranked soldiers up to 40 or 50 times a day in dank brothels, doused with gasoline and burned alive or tied to several horses and torn apart as punishment for resisting or contracting diseases, blown apart from a gun inserted in their vaginas when no longer useful. Shamed, mutilated, some still live to find the courage to tell their stories.

This news item changed the way I read newspapers. It also confronted me with how I divided the world into "us" and "them." When I wrote letters for Amnesty International in response to international injustices and tortures, it was my "us/them" response to suffering. I "felt" the pain of the unjustly imprisoned and the tortured, but they were "them," not "my people."

For the first time I caught an infinitesimal glimpse of the implications of the divided kingdom, the divided house, and the possibilities of world community. We live not in separate houses but in one global house divided against itself. The misery of the Asian women torture victims is my misery. And yes, the brutality of Japanese military men is my brutality. My people. Not in the sense that I own them like the homeowner landlord controls her tenants and the rules they must follow to live in her house. Nor in the sense that they belong to me like my household furniture.

We are one people. As long as we are divided, we cannot stand.

Reflection

With a newspaper before you, slowly and carefully look for an article with a photograph that speaks to your heart. Read the words. Look into the eyes of the people and listen for their stories.

What does it mean to you to think of these people as "your people"?

What are your barriers?

Prayer

Merciful God
Your people are suffering
there on the pages of our
newspapers,
and we read the comics.
Your people
not ours.

Are not "Our people" those who
share
the same genetic makeup,
the same birthplace,
the same sameness?

Your people are our people.
Help us to heal the divisions
we keep making more of:
skin colour, birthplace, faith
expressions,
sexual orientation, gender, body
shape and abilities, income,
age.
Embrace us together
so "them" and "us" are no
longer,
so that differences do not
divisions make.

Wednesday

DID YOU GET IT?

Marilou Carrillo

MARK 4:1-20

"...They have no root and endure only for a while."

The parable of the sower is a painful exercise in categorization and hypocrisy. Seeds, like people, sown in four different places. The seeds sown on the path, eaten by birds: do I belong to the group that doesn't get it because I give up my power and let others take away what is rightfully mine? The seeds that fell on rocky ground: do I belong to the one that *thinks* it gets it, but "when the going gets tough" waves good-bye, "I'm out-a here!"? The seeds that fell among thorns: do I belong to the group that barely has a clue, caught in a system of false security and assumed affluence? The seeds that fell on good soil: or do I belong to the group that "gets it" and actively contributes to a better world?

Do I "have no roots and endure only for a while"? How many intended tasks or attractive short-term projects have I been involved in, only to have my spirit spurt slowly and dissipate aimlessly? So I give up my power and stand immobile because "Satan immediately comes and takes away the word that is sown" in me. I go to a restaurant that feeds the poor on Thanksgiving; or to a movie about the suffering of the colonized Maoris people. Suddenly I am entrenched among the thorns and I didn't even know I had been choked by "the cares of the world and the lure of wealth and the desire for other things."

I want to be sown in good soil. I want to "get it" and be part of transforming and re-creating our communities, our neighbourhoods, our world. While I distract myself in the exercise of categorization, I hear a whisper, "Pssst...let anyone who has ears to hear listen!" (He doesn't mean me.) "Do you not understand this parable? Then how will you understand all the parables?" (He definitely doesn't mean me. I can change and be healed and forgiven.) "Yes, but did you get it?"

This is a parable of discernment. I am the sower and I need to know where I must sow. I will reap what I sow because of where I sow. I need to perceive, understand, and transform, for I carry the seeds wherever I go. I am all of those seeds. I must go where it is life-giving, where the soil is rich and the yield is a hundredfold. Where there is no life, or where there is death, I must depart, flee, turn away. No growth and abundance will be found there.

And so it is that I will keep seeking

in community and finding the place and the people of life. The seeds are numerous. The soil is rich. The yield is overflowing. Did the parable work for me? I pray it did. Did I get it? I pray I can.

REFLECTION RITUAL

Place different types of seeds in an earthen container. Assign to each type of seed a person or situation to which you have been called to respond.

Meditate on:

Discernment of God's spirit in: your daily responses and decisions; hypocrisies and abundance; transformations; life-giving sources for you, others, or a group.

PRAYER

O Creator and Sower of All
Seeds,
Grant us the spirit of humility to
face our daily hypocrisies,
saying one thing and doing
another.
Shower us with grace to receive
your spirit,
to discern where and who we
need to seek,
So we may be honest that you,
and not us,
have the greater knowledge and
power
To plant the seeds of wisdom
and justice
in order to cultivate
life in ourselves and in our
communities;
To hold steadfast when
abundant harvest
requires long struggles and no
immediate result;
As we lie in patient silence and
responsible power
watching and waiting for the
seeds to bring forth life that
feeds all.

Thursday

GLORIFY GOD IN YOUR BODY

Karyn Bigby

1 CORINTHIANS 6:12-20

"Or do you not know that your body is a temple of the Holy Spirit within you, which you have from God, and that you are not your own? For you were bought with a price; therefore, glorify God in your body."

Paul provides us with a powerful image: our bodies as a temple. Writing at a time when some new Christians were practising "paganistic rituals," Paul used this image to appeal to them not to abuse their bodies "...The body is meant not for fornication, but for the Lord, and the Lord for the body." (vs. 13)

As a temple of the Holy Spirit within us, our bodies are sacred. Often we do not treat our bodies that way. Why do we smoke? Why do we take illicit drugs? Why are we promiscuous? Why do we drink alcohol in excess? Why do we prefer to sit on the couch watching television instead of exercising? Why do we eat foods that are harmful to our well-being? Why do we go on starvation diets? Do we not know that our bodies are a temple of the living God? Just as we want to see the corporate body, the church, be in a good state of health, our physical body must also be maintained.

Athletes, whether they be runners, baseball players, or downhill skiers, must strengthen and condition their bodies so that they can be in top shape to achieve peak performance in their respective competitions. Their preparations may include weight training to strengthen their muscles, and practice, practice, practice. The athlete must be both physically and mentally prepared.

Paul's analogy of the body as temple reminds me of athletic shoe commercials. Usually at the centre of focus in these slick advertisements is a perfectly toned man or woman with a physique to be admired. The advertisers' message to us is that their shoes are a necessary component in producing such a fine physique. Society, through the media, often tells us that we have to look like models or the latest action hero. Sometimes this influences us in a negative way, especially those with eating disorders. Teenage girls, the segment who most commonly suffer from these diseases, struggling to look like the models in fashion magazines, do their bodies and their psyche irreparable damage. Maintaining the temple that we call our bodies does not mean that we have to be thin. Whatever our body image, God accepts us for who we are. We do not have to bend to society's view of what we should look like.

REFLECTION

What are we as Christians preparing our bodies for?

How do we prepare ourselves?

What are the necessary components we as Christians need to glorify God with our bodies?

PRAYER

Dear God
We thank you for our physical
being,
for making our bodies a temple
in your Holy Spirit.
Help us to glorify you
by not abusing our bodies.

Friday

SUPPLENESS TO SORROW

Nena Cervantes

GENESIS 43:16-34

He replied, "Rest assured, do not be afraid; your God...must have put treasure in your sacks for you...."

How many of us can see the treasures in a newcomer's sack?

I have always likened sorrow to a pumice stone, a hard, organic instrument that rubs away at callousness to lay bare human sensibilities long hidden by ruthless, self-centred living. Only recently have I discovered, thanks to a Dutch poet, that there is "suppleness to sorrow." Yes, sorrow can mark the face with grace and beauty, like a silken mourning veil draped over the grieving face of a widow. Picture the faces of Jacqueline Kennedy, Coretta King, Corazon Aquino. How did the world respond to these women in their hour of tribulation?

But when sorrow rubs the soul to the core, it injures deeply, twisting the face like a tourniquet. Immigrants from troubled lands sometimes convey sorrow this way. Their faces harden, drawing on-lookers away instead of closer. Some have come to Canada emotionally, psychologically, physically, spiritually raw, their souls a dying ember, craving the life-giving breath of compassion. They have heard the hooves of the four horsemen of the Apocalypse galloping into their villages, and have stared into the macabre faces of war, disease, famine, and death. Can one who has been tortured or raped or seen their children die because there was no more milk to draw from the breast, convey anything but deep sorrow or torment?

Some cannot weep, not out of callousness but because their oppressor's punishment made it physically impossible for their tear ducts to draw tears. Upon his release from prison, Nelson Mandela could not cry because his tear ducts were plugged by alkaline dust floating from rocks he had been forced to break for decades. Yet like so many, he prevailed. The rocks were broken, not he.

Sorrow hardens or softens. When Joseph's brothers abandoned him, they saw the anguish of his soul but still threw him into the pit. Envy hardened them, Joseph's suffering softened him. He conveyed "suppleness of sorrow" when years later he saw his younger brother, Benjamin, and wept in private.

Reflection

When we look into the face or eyes of a stranger, do we throw her or him into a pit?

In what way has sorrow hardened us or given us suppleness to be compassionate?

Prayer

Sorrowing God,
We know pain and we know joy.
We have tasted the bitter and the sweet.
Help us connect with others in their sorrow
as readily as in their happiness.
May our compassion be as a lifeline cast
to those who have fallen in the pit.
Give us courage to lift and be uplifted.

Saturday

Wounded Hearts

Richard Chung-sik Choe

Ezra 3:8-13

"...(the) old people who had seen the first house on its foundations, wept with a loud voice when they saw this house, though many shouted aloud for joy, so that the people could not distinguish the sound of the joyful shout from the sound of people's weeping...."

"Those who have experienced nothing mistake the sound of weeping for singing." (Dahomey Proverb)

How do people gather together to remember the past when there does not seem to be much in common? How do people share their stories without feeling guilty about their feelings about their past? I was asking myself such questions when Moderator Marion Best invited General Council Executive members to reflect on this Ezra passage.

There was much lamentation—about losing the church's influence in society, sadness around "home" churches being shut down due to loss of membership and changing neighbourhoods. When I hear the lamentations of those who have seen the glory of the past, I find it hard to empathize with their loss.

Many ethnic minorities in the church have difficulty remembering the past with fondness. Fifty years ago, Canadian born Japanese Canadian ministers were barred from serving "white" congregations because of their ancestry, except when there was a shortage. Even in such circumstances, they were not allowed to serve communion or officiate at weddings. The past shouts of joy from the status quo have too often drowned out the cries of the pain of the minorities.

But how do we move on from here as one when our stories are so different? when we are coming from such different places? The tears of the status quo have often blinded them from seeing the excitement in the future of the church. Like the younger generation who shouted with joy when they saw the foundation of the Jerusalem Temple, I see hope in the future, not in the past. I strongly believe that our stories of pain and joy are the threads with which our future will be knitted together. When we start sharing our stories, we shall be able to understand what parts have been missing from the whole. I see that as the beginning of intertwining our pasts for the common future. I long for a place where everyone can be heard and have a place. I dream of "a place of radical openness, of recognition and reconciliation, where one could create freely." [8] That place of freedom is the church I dream of.

Reflection

Andrew Sung Park states that "throughout its history, the church has largely overlooked the pain of the victims of sin...the traditional doctrine of sin has been one-sided, seeing the world from the perspective of the sinner only, failing to take account of the victims of sin and injustice."[9] He describes "sin as the volitional act of sinners (oppressors) and Han as the pain of the victim of sin."[10] This Han, Park states, "can be defined as the critical wound of the heart generated by unjust psychosomatic repression, as well as by social, political, economic, and cultural oppression."[11]

What voices are drowning the voices of the pained and the weak in the communities we participate in?

What are sin and "Han" in your life context?

How do we engage with one another in hearing and telling our stories?

Prayer

God of history,
We gather as people of different heritages.
Though we gather as one family,
we share different stories and traditions.
As we remember the past, we confess that
we see more differences than similarities.
We confess that there were times when
we were not able to hear the cries of others.
There were times when we were not able
to join in the celebrations of others.
Help us find ways to listen to one another.
Help us become One as we share our stories.
Help us re-discover that we are all blood relations
through your Son, Jesus Christ.

Part Four - The Spirit Gives Life

3rd Sunday in Lent

FAITH OF A PEOPLE ROOTED IN THE CREATOR

Eleanor Scarlett

JOHN 5:25-29

"Do not be astonished at this; for the hour is coming when all who are in their graves will hear his voice...."

One thing that stood out in my mind while growing up in Jamaica was the faith of the people. They had the trusting faith that Christ speaks of. The people had complete faith that, like Christ, they, too, would experience a resurrection once they left this world.

I remember my paternal grandmother who, like so many other mothers and grandmothers, was illiterate. Yet her faith allowed her to trust in God completely. She would often sing this song:

> "This world is not my own, I am only passing through;
> my treasures are in heaven, somewhere beyond the blue.
> Christ Jesus beckons me and I must surely go.
> I cant stay alone in this world anymore."

People of this culture were not afraid of death. Death for them was the beginning of a new life. During the time of enslavement, the people prayed day and night for death. Death from the Western world would return their spirits to their ancestral home. For them, this would have been true liberation. Death was a welcome event that was celebrated by communities. Today, in these regions, the death of an older person or a community activist is still perceived in this manner. No longer would these people be burdened with the trials and tribulations of this world. Liberation would come because Christ, the source of all life, gives new life to those who die in him.

Some would argue that our people are looking for a "pie in the sky" solution to our problems. People of developing countries work very hard to provide for their basic needs. They know that they cannot trust those in authority to bring about change for them. To effectively bring about any change, they must fully trust in God and believe in the resurrection of the dead. For us, this is hope, real hope.

This will not come easily. No struggle comes without sacrifice. Jesus' struggles led to his death on a cross. There are people aware of this and also prepared to give their lives to bring liberation.

My hope is rooted in a culture that believes in God Who Is, and who will liberate us from our struggles. Christ is the answer. He came to bring new life and to liberate all oppressed peoples from their labours. The scriptures must be fulfilled, and for this we know that one day, if not in this world but in the one to come, liberation will be realized.

REFLECTION

How can liberation be applied to change?

Where is your hope in your culture?

PRAYER

Creator God of all people
help us to experience your liberation.
Enable us as a people to experience your shalom.
Renew in us the faith that once belonged to our foreparents.
May we as a people be able to walk fully assured of your love
that is rooted in Christ, your son,
who gives life to all.

Monday

THE PAIN OF DISCRIMINATION, REJECTION, AND ISOLATION

Alex Kasirye-Musoke

MARK 5:21-43

"She had heard about Jesus and came up behind him in the crowd and touched his cloak. ...Immediately her hemorrhage stopped...."

Have you ever felt that your job application was turned down because of your colour, disability, sex or appearance? Have you ever felt rejected or discriminated against just because of who you are? Have you ever felt that the system to which you belong is working against you?

You are not alone. Many people have felt that way for centuries: refugees, people of colour, the poor, the disabled. Many have been rejected and treated unfairly just because of who they are. Even Jesus suffered rejection, from his village mates as well as from strangers.

Consider women during Jesus' time. They were regarded as unclean compared with men and male children, but even more so during the days of their menstrual period. Although this was a natural phenomenon, a woman and anything she touched or was in contact with during those days was regarded as impure for seven days. She was not allowed to touch anything holy or that which belonged to men, go near any man or enter the sanctuary until the priest, who was always male, performed the procedure of her purification. (Lev.15:19)

A classic example of a woman rejected is the one who suffered hemorrhages for 12 years: 12 years of rejection in a male dominated society because of her sex and condition. She was a sick woman, physically and emotionally. Her self-esteem and confidence had gone. She was poor for she had spent all she had trying to find a cure. She was alienated, isolated, and friendless. All she had was faith in the one who had cured so many. It was this faith that helped her push through the crowd to get to Christ. When she came into contact with him, "she was cured of her troubles."

This is a story about a woman, but it is not just a woman's story. Men can also identify with rejection because of unfair judgement of their skin colour, size or where they have come from. I relate to this story as a man, a Ugandan refugee. Unable to remain in England during a time of extreme racial tensions and unable to return to strife-ridden Uganda, I sought political asylum in Kenya. Kenyans also rejected me and called me "*mukimbizi*" meaning "somebody on the run," somebody who was not Kenyan, somebody who deserved no respect or status. Impure, unclean. Other Ugandan refugees rejected me because I had received higher education in England and was now also culturally different from them. Everywhere I went I was viewed with suspicion as one who was always from somewhere else: from Uganda, from England, from Kenya, from the Anglican church. It was my faith that made me push on despite rejection and discrimination everywhere I turned.

The amazing thing about the hemorrhaging woman's story was that she came out to meet Jesus. She did not sit, hope, and pray that discrimination would one day go away, or fear that her voice would not be heard. She did not remain in hiding, afraid of what Jesus or others would say. This would not have helped her or changed those who discriminated against her. She came knowing he would change her life.

Like the hemorrhaging woman, we all need to move from the periphery, push through the crowd, and touch Jesus' garment. By our faith we will be made well.

REFLECTION

What do you think was the impact of Jesus' words on the woman? On those in the crowd who witnessed this healing?

When has your faith been the source of your healing?

PRAYER

Loving God,
Through faith you give us peace and freedom from our troubles.
Lord, we are troubled by the things we see around us
but we are afraid to speak up.
Give ears to hear, eyes to see, voices to speak,
and hands to heal those who are hurting because of discrimination.
Open our hearts that love may flow to all people.

Tuesday

COMPANIONS ON THE JOURNEY

Kim Uyede-Kai

MARK 6:1-13

"He ordered them to take nothing for their journey except a staff; no bread, no bag, no money in their belts."

A journey without food, money, possessions is a journey from my history, a painful part of Canada's history that wears my face. My feet still walk in the shadow of Japanese Canadians evacuated to internment camps during the Second World War. It was a harrowing journey of displacement, homelessness, blamed victims of racist fears. Forced into the frightening unknown, allowed to take only what they could carry. Never to return to what they left behind. A journey from the past, yet ever present.

My first-born son, Trevor, at 11 years of age, is the same age as my parents were when their families were evacuated. He is a sensitive child, quiet, impressionable, kind and just, with a strong sense of family and home. He is also prone to worry, quick to blame himself when things go wrong, quick to sense another's censure. I wonder how he would have lived through such racial intolerance and displacement.

I wonder how I would have coped

had I been in my grandmothers' place. How could I have packed a whole household into a few small boxes in a couple of weeks, not knowing where we were being sent, or for how long? Would I have been wise enough to choose what was important and necessary? Would I have left behind precious family heirlooms, trusting we would be allowed to return, only to never see them again? Would I have found the strength to leave my home, been able to calm my children's fears, and swallow my own fears and rage at injustice?

Jesus sent out 12 male disciples with only a staff, a solid, sturdy support to lean on. One would assume they were willing to divest themselves of their possessions. Two generations of Japanese Canadians were unwillingly divested on a journey not of their choosing. But they, too, were given a staff. Their "staff" was their dignity, their endurance, their faiths.

And their companions on the journey. Japanese Canadian families and communities journeyed through great hardship, but they did it together. All on the west coast were evacuated. All had homes, businesses, possessions confiscated. All suffered great losses. Many men were separated from their families. Many women were left alone to gather their fractured families and make some semblance of home in the often squalid internment camp ghost towns. At the end of the war, all were forced to relocate east or went to Japan, still homeless. But shared suffering built strong Japanese Canadian communities and strong faiths.

Jesus gave special powers to 12 men and sent them out two by two. He gave them a staff and a companion, and authority over unclean spirits. They were not expected to do God's work on their own power, nor to journey alone. When we are deprived of homes, livelihoods, material possessions, it is in companionship and in faith that we can endure the most frightening journeys.

As I gently teach my son our history, as we work through the racism we still experience today, I am mindful that we, too, are not alone. Thanks be to God.

Reflection

What would you choose to take if you had to pack your entire household into a few small boxes and suitcases, not knowing where you were going, or for how long, or if you would ever return?

When has your journey taken you to a fearful place without material security? What has been your "staff"?

PRAYER

Fearless God,
You send us on journeys into the unknown.
Keep our eyes on the journey,
and not on the unknown.
You send us out without those things which give us security.
Keep our eyes on what you give us,
and not on what we have had to leave behind.
You send us out with a staff to lean on when we need it.
Keep our eyes on our strength,
on how far we can go,
and not on how weak we are
because we need support.

You send us to walk with a companion.
Keep our hearts on the shared vision,
hope and healing,
and not on the shared hardship.
Help us to go where you send us.

Wednesday

ILLITERACY AS DEATH AND LIFE

Marilou Carrillo

2 CORINTHIANS 2:14-3:6

"...for the letter kills, but the Spirit gives life."

As I sit and write, meditating on Paul's letter to the Corinthians, I am struck by how I take for granted my ability to write. This self-expression is part of who I am, a vital component of my identity; this privilege of reading and writing, growing up in middle class Manila, where "middle class" is a denial of the two class tiers in the Philippines of rich and poor. I painfully recall the unnamed women, the wives of construction workers who worked for my father, the young women snatched from their homes in the rural areas to work in city homes, and the women on the streets, bent doing laundry or carrying babies on their hips while working. None knew how to read and write.

I remember Juana in a Guatemalan refugee camp asking me to send a message to her friend now living in Vancouver. "Even if I cannot write a letter, tell her I am not well but surviving, and I am happy to hear she and her family are well." On my return to Vancouver, I shared a photograph and Juana's message, but not her feelings, her warm smile nor open heart, her poverty nor strength of survival, not her own written words.

Paul insists that our competence comes from God and, therefore, all of us are competent to be ministers. I think of the profound competence of poor women to minister to their families, relatives, and community friends. Yet they struggle day by day to survive. Their illiteracy kills them and their children, for the link between poverty and illiteracy is staggering.

The rich are not illiterate. The poor are. Two-thirds of them are women, and along with illiterate men, comprise around 900 million people who cannot express themselves nor receive understanding in the written word. Yet educating women not only improves their quality of life, it also reduces infant mortality and family size, and improves health and productivity of the entire family. To read and write is to choose and give life.

Poor, urban women are on the faculty of a Women's Studies Center in Manila, teaching others and sharing their competence. They understand the spirit of God's law in the context of their lives. They have many stories which we need to hear. These women are ministers of the new covenant. They have started base communities in Latin America, Asia, and Africa. They have used the Bible as their tool for analysis. They have taken the "spirit of the new covenant" and transformed the written word into the love of God, unmediated by written language. The word is their lives, and their stories are witnesses to the Spirit that gives life. Illiteracy can also be a source of life, a blessing for the rich and the literate.

Reflection

Write the words "confidence, competence, ministers, new covenant, the letter kills, Spirit gives life" on separate pieces of paper. Take one of these pieces of paper. Think of a person from the Two-Thirds World whom you have met or read about. How would this person express or teach you the profound meaning or spirit of this word or phrase? What is one thing you have learned or can learn from him/her?

Reflect on the relationship between illiteracy that kills and illiteracy that gives life.

Meditate on the competence of poor, illiterate persons as ministers of God.

Prayer

O Source of All Wisdom,
Who wrote on the tablets of
stone with your finger,
Protect and defend those who
cannot enter your halls of
literacy.
Grant them competence to speak
your words of truth.
Give them food, shelter, health,
and work.
Give them life.
O Teacher of Justice,
Who read from the scroll of
Isaiah and who bent down
and wrote on the ground,
Stand by those who work with
their hands and tell their
stories.
Grant them confidence as they
risk and struggle daily.
Give them paper, pencils, books,
and teachers from which to
learn.
Give them life.

Thursday

Personal Sacrifice

Karyn Bigby

Mark 6:30-46

"But he answered them, 'You give them something to eat.'"

Have you ever, after a hard day's work, just wanted to go home and relax? And then has your boss asked you to work overtime? Did you stay?

This must have been the same dilemma the disciples found themselves in as they searched for a quiet place to get away from the crowds. Instead, Jesus asked the disciples to help find food for the very people they wanted to dismiss.

Just as Jesus was willing to forgo his needs for the greater good, so, too, did Nelson Mandela in his struggle against apartheid. On June 19, 1990, my home congregation, Union United Church in Montreal had the pleasure of receiving the Mandelas as part of their North American tour after Nelson Mandela's release from jail. The Rev. Dr. E. Leicester Bigby marvelled at Mr. Mandela's 1985 refusal to accept conditional release from prison. During his welcoming remarks, Dr. Bigby quoted Nelson Mandela's own prophetic words:

"I cherish my own freedom dearly, but I care even more for your freedom....I cannot sell my birthright, nor am I prepared to sell the birthright of the people to be free....I am in prison as the representative of the people and your organization, the African National Congress, which was banned....Your freedom and mine cannot be separated. I will return...."

This was not Nelson Mandela's own personal struggle. The abolition of apartheid was the goal of many. Nor did Mandela's mission end with his release. The day he was set free, he called for his people to "seize the moment, so that the process toward democracy is rapid and uninterrupted."

What did Nelson Mandela sacrifice? As a freedom fighter, he sacrificed more than the 27 years he spent in prison. Prior to his imprisonment, he had already given up time with his family and spent time away from his legal practice. The greatest sacrifice of all was his personal freedom, limited that it was in the apartheid practised in South Africa.

What was gained? On April 27, 1994, the first national, nonracial, one-person-one-vote elections were held. No longer could the minority whites make all the decisions for the majority, most of whom are Black.

Who gained? That depends on who is answering the question. To some whites who supported the status quo, they did not gain anything. To some Blacks, they did not gain nearly enough.

What distinguishes Nelson Mandela from many is the great personal sacrifice he made for his fellow human beings and his ability to forgive his captors.

Let us not forget those in South Africa, but also remember those persons throughout the world who sacrificed their very lives for their people.

Reflection

How much would you personally be willing to sacrifice for the good of your neighbour?

What sacrifices do you make in your own life?

Prayer

God,
Thank you, for all the sacrifices
people make for one another:
selfless parents,
caregivers of sick or elderly
relatives,
those who suffered that we

might live.
We thank you for the life and
death of Jesus,
the ultimate sacrifice.
Help us seize the life and
opportunity
bought for us at so great a cost.

Friday

WELCOME STRANGER

Nena Cervantes

MARK 7:1-23

"Then he called to the crowd again and said to them, 'Listen to me, all of you, and understand: there is nothing outside a person that by going in can defile, but the things that come out are what defile.'"

"How can our congregation be more welcoming?" This is a question which arises often in my church. Many answers have been offered to resolve the problem, but the issue remains like lint on an impeccably tailored suit.

A woman in the congregation recalled how welcome she felt as a newcomer to a church in England because a member of the congregation brought a cake to her doorstep. To her, it was a welcoming gesture, an act she offered as a possible solution to make newcomers in the church feel at home.

To me her story had many assumptions: that she and the baker of the cake shared similar ethnicity, the same culture, the same roots, and theology. She was an English rose being repotted into English soil, albeit in a different county.

Often today's newcomer to a church in Toronto is being transplanted into a new country not just a new county. The cake the newcomer may feel at home with may be made of rice instead of wheat. But whatever the physical substance of the offering of welcome, ingesting the cake will not defile the newcomer. What might defile that person is the look he or she sees the very first time he or she locks gazes with a long-standing member of the church: a look which unconsciously says, "Welcome, you are family. Let us share everything equally;" or, "Welcome, passerby, when are you leaving?"

Rejection defiles because it separates giver from receiver like a rotten egg thrown into a tasty cake batter. Acceptance unites. A cake offered with rejection at heart is offered on a broken vessel. It is not what the hands proffer, but what the eyes say that matter, for they truly are the windows to our souls.

REFLECTION

What are our assumptions when we welcome newcomers? What are the things which defile?

What or who makes us kindred spirits?

PRAYER

Loving Spirit,
Guide us to our secret garden
where our spirit blooms like
magnolias,
dogwood, and lilacs in perennial
spring.
Help us find one elating moment
in our past
when we felt connected with
You,
to pluck that memory and offer
it to a newcomer,
the spirit of welcome shining
brightly in our eyes,
So that they, too, may grow
a secret garden of their own.

Saturday

AGAINST THE WIND

Richard Chung-sik Choe

MARK 6:47-56
"When (Jesus) saw that (the disciples) were straining at the oars against an adverse wind, he came towards them...walking on the sea....They thought it was a ghost and cried out; for they...were terrified. But immediately he spoke to them and said, 'Take heart, it is I; do not be afraid.'"

Pictures at an exhibition: flowers, butterflies, houses at the foot of a mountain, people strolling in the park. These are the pictures you might see in a glossy picture book. They are a collection of artwork done by children. The difference is that these drawings are from the Nazi concentration camp in former Czechoslovakia called Terezin. Terezin, known also in German as Theresienstadt, was a "model ghetto" for the "privileged Jews" during the Second World War.

An artist named Friedl Dicker-Brandeis was ordered to Theresienstadt in December 1942. It is said that "she conceived a mission for herself and brought what art materials she could to the camp."[12] She began to go around from group to group, teaching children art for free. Her method of teaching was peculiar. She would tell stories to children, and the children were required to draw objects she would mention twice in her story. The children not only drew objects, but also their inner worlds and the horrible realities they were experiencing. Friedl Dicker-Brandeis was able to touch the lives of the children and help calm their terrifying existence. About 15,000 children under the age of 15 passed through the Terezin concentration camp between 1942-1944. Of these, less than 100 survived. Friedl Dicker-Brandeis was deported to Auschwitz on October 6, 1944, and died in Birkenau. She was the wounded healer of Terezin.

Sometimes our life is like straining at the oars against an adverse wind. As I was reading the story of Friedl Dicker-Brandeis, I began to think, could I be like her—could I be like Jesus—to those who are in need of help? Would I be able to find purpose in life even when my life had turned for the worse?

> "I've met enough people.
> Seldom a human being.
> Therefore, I will wait
> until my life's purpose
> is fulfilled
> and you will come.

Though there is anguish
deep in my soul
what if I must search for you
forever?
I must not lose faith,
I must not lose hope."[13]

- Alena Synkova, a child from Terezin

REFLECTION

Picture the scene as you read Mark 6:47-56 in silence.

Can you remember a time when you were struggling against the adverse wind in your life? Did you encounter someone who was able to be with you and calm your fear?

What images and issues come to you as you read the poem by Alena Synkova?

Who was she waiting for?
Was it you?

PRAYER

God of compassion,
I search for your presence
as I experience violence in and
around me.
Could I ever dare to be like you,
I wonder?
Would I be able to imagine
flowers and butterflies,
instead of weapons of
destruction?
Would I be able to speak words
of love and compassion
instead of hatred and self-
centredness?
Would I be bold enough to
dream of a world
where I could be brother or
sister to those I meet?

O God,
empower me to work for a
peaceful world,
enable me to be your
spokesperson and
encourage me to dream your
dreams
with those I meet.

Part Five - Unexpected Blessings

4th Sunday in Lent

Unconditional Blessings

Eleanor Scarlett

Genesis 48: 8-22
"And he said, 'Bring them to me, please, that I may bless them.'"

In the Hebrew scripture, only the male children receive the blessings. In most cultures, this same practice continues even today. It is important to know that no one is denied the blessing that God gives. In the Gospel of John, Christ reminds us that God offers eternal life to everyone. This is the greatest of all blessings. If we are God's children, then God's blessings belong to us.

It is a wonderful sense of security to know that God is not like humankind and treats us all equally regardless of our race, class, gender or economic status. Everyone can come to the waters and drink of God's blessing; it is given freely to each and every one of us. God's love is unconditional. It is out of this love for us that we were given the blessings of God's son who lived and shared our pains and sorrows.

As we journey through this lenten season, may we become aware now more than ever, that had it not been for Christ, most of us would never experience God's blessings. Christ's death on the cross brought about his resurrection. It is this resurrection that reconciles us as people of faith into accepting God's blessings, whereby we are able to walk humbly, knowing that our Saviour walks with us.

Reflection
What are the things which make you secure?

How do you experience God's blessings through Christ?

Prayer

God of all blessings,
we give you thanks today more
than ever
for the gift of Your Son Jesus.
Christ has blessed us in so many
ways
and for this we are thankful.
We ask that You send Your
Spirit upon us,
so that we will become closer to
You,
especially during this lenten
season.

Monday

ENFOLDED IN LOVE

Richard Chung-sik Choe

GENESIS 49:1-28

"...Blessings of heaven above, blessings of the deep that lies beneath, blessings of the breasts and of the womb."

The entire five floors of Sam Poong Department Building collapsed in South Korea in July, 1995. It was the most expensive and luxurious department store in South Korea. It was also a house of cards built on greed and disregard for human life. A greedy owner with strong ties to the military dictatorship, an unconscionable builder, and corrupt officials in the late 1980s had constructed a building that was to crumble during the busiest hour of the day.

Hundreds perished in the debacle of the collapse, yet some survivors were found 13, 14, and 17 days later, in extreme summer heat without food or water, still pinned under the weight of what used to be five stories filled with merchandise. An amazing and moving miracle. Yet one story in the newspaper touched me far deeper and moved me to tears.

Rescuers found the body of an elderly woman under the rubble as they were excavating the disaster area. They looked closer to discover a child wrapped in her skirt. Officials later identified the bodies as those of a four-year old girl and her grandmother who was in her 80s.

Even when faced with a suffering death, this grandmother's love enabled her to comfort the child in this horrible situation by enfolding her beloved grandchild in her skirt. This grandmother's love and this child's response of faith in her grandmother's comforting love was a miracle.

The image of a selfless grandmother stirs memories of my own grandmother (*halmoni* in Korean) who lives in South Korea. My halmoni was a refugee of the Korean War. All of my father's family members had to flee their homes in North Korea during the Korean War in the early 1950s. My well-educated grandfather, suddenly a refugee, had difficulty coping with forced dislocation. When he became crippled by his loss and his battered pride, it was my grandma who carried the family through the war years. She took charge of the family and gave it a life once again. She unceasingly believed in a bright future ahead no matter what the circumstances.

Since my army officer father had to move around quite often, I grew up with my grandparents. I remember how Halmoni used to wait by the school gate every lunch time. No matter how cold the winter, no matter how foul the weather, she would walk the long distance to my school with a hot lunch for me. I learned from my father that she did the same for him during the early 1950s when he was incarcerated on an island as a male war refugee, waiting for his credentials to be cleared by the military police.

My grandfather blessed me with his love of mythical stories. Halmoni's blessing to me was the blessing of unconditional love, faith, and acceptance without any conditions attached. She gave all she had: her love as a grandmother, mother and wife, and an undying spirit.

A grandmother blesses her child with her love and comfort even as she is dying under concrete rubble. Perhaps that was what was happening to Jacob and his sons in the Genesis passage. Even on his deathbed Jacob worries about each of his children and blesses them with a suitable blessing. Such is the love we still experience at times through our family relations. Such is the love given to us by God.

Reflection

What have been the blessings of your ancestors, your family?

When have you been enfolded in blessing? When have you enfolded another?

Prayer

Loving God,
In our deepest suffering
you work miracles.
Continue to bless us with your
unconditional love.
Teach us to respond to your love
with a trusting faith.

Tuesday

FULL OF STORY

Kim Uyede-Kai

MARK 8:1-10
"They ate and were filled...."

"My oldest friend died," was my seven-year old son, Jeremy's sad contribution to his grade two class sharing time. "She was part of our family." Margaret Livey had been 86-years old and had indeed been Jeremy's friend. He had loved her as family. In the months following her death, we spoke of her often. We remembered her kindness to "two of her favourite boys," my sons: her cards and gifts at Christmas and Easter, her treats for any occasion, her interest in their lives. We remembered her loving openness to amalgamating her beloved century old congregation with our 32-year old English language Japanese Canadian congregation; her passionate devotion to the familiar old church she grew up in and equally to the new, blended church she grew old in. And we remembered her crooked house.

Margaret's house was old and its flooring had shifted severely after major construction across the street. A walk in her house was either uphill or downhill. Still, on our first visit to her house, I was mortified when Jeremy's first reaction to the sharply sloped floor was to drop to the rug and roll like a log from one end of the room to the other. Margaret just smiled and told him that sometimes she felt like rolling too. Then she told us stories about how her house came to be so crooked and what it had been like when the floors were straight.

Margaret was an engaging story-teller and had a story for every occasion, because every occasion was a story. She talked about people she knew, about her family, her church. She talked about her computer which she learned to use when she was 80. Each new learning was a story. She did not just live in the past but for the present and the future.

Her last years of life were a physical struggle as her health deteriorated. She moved to an apartment with a level floor, but her struggle to stay well was increasingly more uphill than down. Still, she had stories to tell to loving listeners.

Margaret's stories have ended now. Her earthly life has ended. There are no more new stories. Or are there? In the re-telling of her old stories, I keep being surprised by the new life and new meaning I find in them. Her church lives on without her, yet her love for its life and growth continues to fuel its future. Her old, crooked house is not just an amusing reminiscence, but a story that gives birth to new stories in new contexts, like this one. Stories of faith and the faithful do not just live in the past, but live on into the future. Just as the seven loaves and a few fish that fed the four thousand can continue to feed us many times over in new and different ways.

After her memorial service, we remembered Margaret as we ate the shortbread we had bought but were unable to give to her before she died. We remembered, told stories, ate, and were filled. Filled with shortbread; filled with Margaret's life stories; filled with her love of God; filled with Love.

REFLECTION

Think of a meal when you had been "filled" with more than the meal. Remember the company or the occasion; remember the food, the conversation.

Tell stories of your remembrances as stories for today, not just "the good old days."

PRAYER

Endless Story God,
You fill our lives with story,
Your Story
Glorious, rich, ordinary, life-
giving.
Why, then, do we think
stories are for the children
for living in fantasy worlds,
or for the simple-minded
for living in shallowness,
or for the old people
for living in the past?
Why not for mature, intellectual
adults
who need food of higher
learning?
Teach us to eat of the food that
is story.
Help us to keep the stories alive,
to honour the Life and Truth
in Your story
and the story-teller.

Wednesday

WOMAN WAITING TO BE STONED

Marilou Carrillo

JOHN 7:53-8:11

"Neither do I condemn you."

Under the Hudood Ordinances promulgated by General Zia ul Haq in 1979, a woman or girl who reports a rape is liable to find herself accused of the serious offence of *zina*—adultery. The rape survivor is assumed guilty of "illicit sexual intercourse" unless she can prove her innocence. This requires producing, as witnesses to the act, four Muslim adult males of good character.

In 1984 a 15-year old parentless girl call Jehan Mina was raped by her uncle and her cousin while staying at their home to tend her sick aunt. Later, when she showed signs of pregnancy, she confessed to a relative that the rape had occurred. He went to the police and a case was set in motion.

When the case came to trial, the accused men were acquitted. Not surprisingly there were no "four adult male witnesses" to the crime. And the court found that the men could not be punished merely on the basis of Jehan Mina's statement. Her pregnancy was seen as a confession of *zina* and she was sentenced to 100 lashes, the maximum penalty.

On appeal the sentence was mitigated to three year's imprisonment and 10 lashes. She was not acquitted because the court found it unsatisfactory that she had waited until her pregnancy became apparent to make the accusation against her uncle.

Jehan Mina served her sentence and gave birth to her child in jail. Although no woman has since been sentenced to the maximum penalty for adultery, the number of imprisonments under the Hudood Ordinances is rising: 738 in 1990, compared to 503 in 1984.[14]

The jagged edges of these stones cut through my feet. I massaged them with scented lotion just last night and noticed the dry cracks on my heels. He liked my feet and ignored the black crevices of caked mud hardened by the miles I walked to see him.

The stinging beneath my toes let out a scream only I could hear. Where is my bed? Last night, its softness and pillows of feather nestled my head. What taunting voice jeers at me? They wish me dead! And I will die in just an interminable while. Who saw us? Who told them?

No! I can't die! I walked and hid in the shadows for months, but last night...he clasped me in the dark. The cries of crickets echoed my longing for an embrace in the loneliness of night. What? The taunting voice calls now for him? Who is this man bent from that wooden stool?

The stick he holds draws a spiral, moving inwards among the stones and mud and dust. He arches his back, straightens his neck, and utters something to them. Can I enter his spiral? And burrow my aching body into the ground? What? The spiral now moves outwards! I cannot follow it. I cannot come out from the underground.

His head moves slowly upward as the stick rises from the ground. He turns to me and draws my gaze to him. His lips begin to move, "Has everyone left?" I nod and awaken the raw stab wounds on my feet as I shift my body erect.

"Has no one condemned you?" My lips, scorched and sealed, draw precious breath through them. "No one, sir." He rises from the stool and drops the stick beside his feet. His feet, dusty and beaten, take a step towards me. I step back and limp over a large stone broken in half. "Nor do I condemn you."

His finger points to the spiral underneath his feet. "Go and be free," rings clearly through my bruised body, as he turns and walks away behind me.

REFLECTION

Place two stones in your place of reflection. One stone represents the stone that is still today being used to kill women for "crimes" committed. The other represents the cornerstone, the one that holds the structure's integrity.

Meditate on:

- Jehan Mina's relative who believed her and Jesus who did not judge the woman;
  (How were they the same? different?)
- a stone used as an instrument of violence; as an instrument of creation and of peace;
- the duality of these stones and what they represent, created and originating from One Source.

PRAYER

O Origin of All Existence,
Give us your strength to know
  that evil and goodness
  belong in this universe.
Guide us lest we dash our foot
  against the stone.
Take us to that place of Mystery
  where what is not
  understood
becomes unity and stillness.
For you have said we must be
  still
and know that you are God.

Thursday

STRENGTH IN UNITY

Karyn Bigby

1 CORINTHIANS 12:12-26
"For just as the body is one and has many members, and all the members of the body, though many, are one body, so it is with Christ. For in the one Spirit we were baptized into one body—Jews or Greeks, slaves or free—and we were all made to drink of one Spirit."

As a child, my father would tell this story:

> A father had three sons. One day, he gave each son a stick. They were each told to break their stick in two. This they did very easily. The father gave them each another stick, identical to the first. He asked them to put their sticks together. They were now asked to break them. They each tried to break the bundle of sticks and failed. Their strength was in unity.

What is the moral of this story? By cooperating and working together we can only be stronger, just as the strength of the sticks increased when bound together.

The church is made up of a multiplicity of cultures and races. We are like flowers growing in a garden. Some are daisies, some roses, and others azaleas. Each flower is unique yet as all the flowers in the garden grow, together they make the most beautiful sight. Imagine a garden with only daisies. Sure, they are pretty, but imagine how much more interesting the garden becomes as we add other flowers.

Are we, as a church, just a garden of daisies, a melting pot of cultures? Or are we a brilliant celebration of textures, patterns, and colours, a true mosaic?

My home church was formed over 80 years ago when many churches in the city of Montreal refused to accept Blacks. Often they were relegated to the back of the church or were not welcome at all. Prejudice still exists, but people are becoming more attuned to each other's differences.

At Union United Church the congregation is comprised of people from varying cultural backgrounds, even though most share a common skin colour. It is a vibrant congregation because people work together. Once a year we hold Heritage Week and celebrate each other's cultures through various activities. In February, Black History Month, we learn about each other's stories. Celebration of who we are as a people is ongoing.

There was a time at Union when the congregation segmented into various groups: Nova Scotians, Jamaicans, Trinidadians, Barbadians, and so on. Through events and celebrations, the people realized that their strength increased by working together.

Within the wider church community, Blacks and other minority groups struggle to have their voices heard. Their stories and gifts are the different flowers which enrich the garden of the church and society. When we all work together, we can accomplish many things. This is what Paul had in mind when he wrote about all as being one body and the importance of each member.

REFLECTION

How can we as a church work together?

As we share the same soil, rain and sun, how can we "grow" together in unity in this garden we call "church"?

PRAYER

God, we are your family,
your carefully tended garden
with a multiplicity of glorious
foliage and blossoms.
Help us to feel that we all belong
even when we are not all the
same.
Help us to treat others as if they,
too, belong,
because we share the same life-
giving elements.

Friday

BURNING BUSHES

Nena Cervantes

EXODUS 2:23- 3:15

"Then Moses said, 'I must turn aside and look at this great sight, and see why the bush is not burned up.'"

I've always wondered what it would be like to see the burning bush, not content to see Charlton Heston descend from Mt. Sinai as hoary-haired Moses.

As I part the curtain of time, I realize that I did see the angel of the Lord appear in a flame of fire out of the midst of bushes. We had just flown from Manila to a small town in the southern part of the Philippines. It was past midnight. Several cars met our party and formed a caravan which headed toward the hotel. We had to drive beyond paved roads onto dirt roads. We prayed before the journey, knowing we might be ambushed.

Trees and bushes lined either side of the road. Above the firmament was sky, like jet velvet encrusted with lustrous diamonds. Around us, crickets and cicadas chirped dull refrains.

The slow motion of the cars was lulling us all to sleep when suddenly, just beyond, lay rows of trees and a sight the like of which we had never seen before. A gasp was all any of us city slickers could muster. All the trees were aflame with a soft glow!

Every leaf of every branch, of every tree was covered with fireflies. The drivers astutely slowed the cars to muffle the noise, but the fireflies had begun to stir. I could not tell whether the Milky Way had descended or whether we had ascended to the stars. Fatigue waned. For that brief moment we were at one with the universe. Here *am* I, thought I, exalting.

"And when the Lord saw that he had turned aside to see, God called to him out of the bush, 'Moses, Moses!' And he said, 'Here I am.'"

REFLECTION

When have you felt Divine presence in nature?

What made that experience extraordinary?

How did you express thankfulness?

PRAYER

Divine Spirit,
Great Giver of life,
the earth and its fullness belong
to You.
Remind us to respect it.
Help us to adore the many
creatures
which endow this planet with
unique splendour.

Saturday

REASON TO GO ON

Richard Chung-sik Choe

MARK 9:2-13

"Then a cloud overshadowed them, and from the cloud there came a voice, 'This is my Son, the Beloved; listen to him!'"

It is not easy to go on living if there is nothing to live for. There are times in our lives when we find it very hard—almost impossible—to go on living the way we have been. It might be because of the relationship we are in, a career that is leading us nowhere, or because we find life very lonely—carrying too many scars from life, no one really seeming to care for us.

Leaving South Korea as a teenager has been a source of pain and anger for me for many years. I was uprooted from the world I was born into and thrown onto strange soil. I did not know how deep my pain and anger went until I began to share them with my friends at seminary. Ever since I came to Canada I felt inadequate—inadequate about the English language, Canadian customs, everything that comes with being a stranger. I constantly felt that I was just not good enough at anything I did. I was uncertain about my future in Canada as well. How does one live in a country when one cannot express oneself? How does one plan for a future when nothing around makes one feel at home? Yet at the same time, I searched for a voice of warmth and acceptance as I struggled through.

I remember my first Sunday in a Korean Canadian church. It was around Christmas time and a friend of mine had been pestering me to attend his church. Although I was not really happy about the hour long sermon or the equally long prayers that began with the story of creation and ended with Jesus being the Alpha and the Omega, I felt at home in its warmth and comfort. I heard God's voice telling me that I was indeed loved by God. That particular church at that particular time was a place of belonging for recent Korean immigrants. Everyone felt and acted like members of a close, extended family.

Growing up in Canada as a minority has not been an easy experience. However, making friends of people with different backgrounds and life experiences has been an amazing source of hope and grace and blessing.

When the disciples were confused and fearful of their future as friends of Jesus, they heard the voice of God resonating from the depth of their being. Each one of us is a friend of Jesus. We are also called to be friends to those we meet in our life journeys.

REFLECTION

What are your scars and your anger?

What helps you to move on?

With whom do you talk when you are disillusioned?

Where do you find a sense of hope when you are troubled?

PRAYER

God of hope,
there are times when we feel so alone.
There are times when we cannot find a reason to go on.
We seek your transforming presence
as we take time to look into our hearts....
(*spend a few minutes opening your heart to God*)
These are our fears and uncertainties.
Transform our fears into confidence.
Help us to discern your purpose in our life.
In Jesus' name, we pray.

Part Six - United and Uniting

5th Sunday in Lent

Gifts Given

Eleanor Scarlett

Exodus 3:16-4:12

"But Moses said to the Lord, 'O my Lord, I have never been eloquent, neither in the past nor even now that you have spoken to your servant; but I am slow of speech and slow of tongue.'"

We live in a world which tells us everything should be perfect. The perfect child, the perfect spouse, the perfect I.Q., the perfect job.

Moses deviated from the norm of perfection. Yet God saw in him what no one else could have seen. God is able to see within each and every one of us what no human being can see. We are all given gifts; every one of us. We, at times, find great difficulty in exercising these gifts.

My girl friend, Grace, was a rare person who was multi-talented, especially in music and sciences. She sang, composed music and lyrics, played the piano and guitar, and taught mathematics and sciences. Yet her greatest gift was in her smile. She had a special smile that left a lasting impression on all who knew her. She was called by God to minister to the sick and broken-hearted; she challenged the status quo of society. Yet she remained humble; her love for her family and friends, community of faith, and her career remain as a memorial to her life.

God knows the gifts we have. God enables us to use these gifts. There are times when we are not even aware of the gifts we have, yet others are drawn to us in ways beyond our initiating. There are times when we are called by God to use our gifts in areas where we do not feel worthy; yet when we respond to these calls, we can make a difference in someone's life and in our own.

I was called into ministry in my youth. In many ways, I can relate to Moses. I felt inadequate. Despite working in many areas with the church, I still believed that I was not good enough to carry out God's work of ordered ministry. I knew within my heart what God required of me, yet I could not do it. I went on to other career paths. There was still that longing, yet I continued to resist even as I used my gifts in psychiatric nursing. Finally, I could no longer run from God's call to ordered ministry. Today as a theology student, my life is blooming spiritually. As recipients of gifts, we must continue to listen to God's call to nurture them in order that they might grow, sometimes in ways we wouldn't choose ourselves.

Reflection

How are you discerning your God-given gifts?

How are you using them? How are you not using them?

Prayer

God of Moses, and of Aaron and
Miriam,
Speak to us in our imperfections,
in our giftedness, in our
resistance.
Be in our mouths and teach us
what we are to speak and
do,
in Your service.

Monday

Ambassadors of Christ

Alex Kasirye-Musoke

Exodus 4:10-20

"But Moses said, 'O my Lord, please send someone else.'"

Moses was mistaken. He thought he needed to be superhuman to do the assignment God had given him. He could not see himself going into Pharaoh's magnificent palace, let alone asking him for the release of the Israelites. "Can't you find someone better to send, Lord? Look at me, a poor man. I am not a public speaker or a diplomat. I stammer when I speak. How can I address Pharaoh? What words shall I use? And look at what I am wearing; it is not formal garb to go to a palace. I am not eloquent and therefore cannot be a leader." Moses recognized and capitalized on his inadequacies so much that he could not see himself rising to the level of God's ambassador.

Many of us tend to be like Moses. We shy away from God's call, responsibility, and service, and make excuses. Moses's call can be an eye opener for us. We become aware that God's work is best done by people who think they are not fit for it. In many cases, those with all the advantages and gifts fail. This could be because they are too glib, too efficient, too robust, or too sure of themselves to be open to God's leading and to articulate God's message in the simplest way possible. It is amazing what God can do through us when we acknowledge our weakness and say, like Isaiah, "Lord, here I am. Send me."

I am an African immigrant for whom English is a foreign language. When God called me to be a United Church minister responsible for a pastoral charge, I protested. Although I have all the academic qualifications, I was apprehensive because of my limited knowledge of English, my accent, and lack of a "Caucasian" sense of humour. Being a visible racial minority and the only one of my kind in the entire Conference, I thought I could not manage to preach and touch souls. I never looked at myself as an ambassador of Christ. Having come from a little rural church in Africa, I feared the size and grandeur of the church in which I was asked to minister. As I read this passage today, it spoke to me in a very special way. In it I could see not Moses but myself, pleading with God, "Who am I that I should be minister at this magnificent church? Lord, send someone else."

God has since shown me there is something deeper and more wonderful in me than just my skin colour, my accent, my size, and words. God has given me a message to carry and God's presence within has blessed me. Each day God's promise, "I will help your speech and tell you what to say," has come to pass. Each Sunday people have said, "You have done it again; this was even better than last Sunday." My response always is, "God has done it."

We are all ambassadors of Christ. All we need to do is say, "Here I am Lord, send me" and God will give us the words and the power.

Reflection

When did you ever feel called to serve God in any capacity?

What was your response?

If the call were repeated today, how would you respond?

Prayer

Serving God,
give us the grace to follow in the steps of Jesus,
who came among us as one who serves.
May we spend and be spent serving you and one another,
the poor, the hungry, the weak, the sick, and the dying.

May we work with faith,
strength, and courage
for the liberation of the
oppressed and the
restoration of dignity and
freedom
to all people, of those created in
your own image. In Jesus'
name.

Tuesday

The Peace of Order

Kim Uyede-Kai

1 Corinthians 14:20-33a
"…For God is a God not of disorder but of peace."

My house is a mess. Every now and then, fed up with tripping over month old forts and mazes made from unlikely sundry household items, I go on a ranting and raving cleaning rampage. Especially when company is coming and *their* house is always immaculate. My children don't like to be barked at, but they like mess. Besides, they think things dropped on the floor transmutate into carpet fibres. How else could they be rendered invisible to the person who dropped them?

Technically, as a "stay-at-home" mother with only occasional paying work and both sons in school full days, I should have time for housework. No, my priorities have been ordered differently for me. Scrubbing the floor gets put off yet again because a tight writing deadline must be met. Supper is delayed because a song on the stereo calls for immediate dancing and singing with my children. Extra shopping trips are needed to celebrate reading the end of a well-loved book by cooking a special meal of the foods mentioned in the story, and dressing up as a favourite character. And a rubber vampire bat and a glow-in-the-dark snake dwell in the cluttered bathroom first aid drawer because that is the darkest room in the house.

I often despair that I am doomed to live a life of frustrating disorder in my house. How could there be any peace in such chaos?

So I look to the writings of Vietnamese Zen master, Thich Nhat Hanh. His book, *Peace is Every Step*, is such a tranquil pause that I no longer see the candy wrappers hidden under the sofa or the dust bunnies rising in glee every time someone walks by. Thich says that peace is not the ultimate destination at the end of a life's journey, but to be found in every breath, every step along the way. Peace is not a commodity that will come to us from outside of ourselves, but is within and always there.

But of course! What I see as disordered mess and a hindrance to peace is an external expectation of order. There is peace in unbridled creativity and in companionship. "Ten hugs a day," my youngest child's rule, are more important than rushing out the door to be on time for a meeting. Order the home, not the house, and we will experience the God of peace.

As we were taking our first bites of dinner, a neighbour, locked out of his house on an unseasonably cold evening, knocked on the door. Cold and worried because his family should have been home, he deserved no less than us bundling up, leaving our warm house and our barely touched meal, and driving him to look for his family. Returning later, I ploughed a path to the telephone so he could make some calls, during which time his family arrived home safely. What peace there can be after, or in spite of, an hour of chaos in a messy house.

A messy house? My house only looks like it is in disorder. In fact, its human inhabitants live very ordered lives. If I can make my home a nurturing place where peace can grow, I have order and I will find peace in all the mess. Even with a vampire bat and a snake in the first aid drawer.

REFLECTION

Where is the messiest part of your house (for some this may be less difficult to identify than for others)? What do you do to bring order to it?

What brings order to the messiest part of your life? Where is there peace in it?

PRAYER

God, somehow you get through
to us
in the clutter of our lives,
in the clutter of our prayers.
Sometimes spending time with
you is like
picking clothes off the floor,
putting away winter coats before
summer's end,
cleaning the toaster crumb tray,
vacuuming the refrigerator coils,
And the feeling of satisfaction
that the time spent was
worthwhile.
Until the clutter begins again
as quickly as static cling
sucks together the clothes
left in the dryer too long,
Teach us to find peace along the
way,
ordered within us
not disordered from without.

Wednesday

TRANSFORMATION AS A CONCRETE EVENT

Marilou Carrillo

MARK 7: 24-30

"Now the woman was a Gentile, of Syro-phoenician origin."

This is a story in the Christian narrative where Jesus is transformed by a direct encounter, by a woman from a non-dominant group. This story, like the lives and stories of racial-ethnic women, has been hidden from view and far from hearing range. People from other races and cultures are often rendered invisible when negative stereotypes surface. Even Jesus was content to respond to her powerless posture defined by generations and years of historical domination by his social group. Today we would call this racism, "prejudice plus power." Because of her belief in her very existence and in life for her child, the Syro-phoenician woman stood on a different ground. She did not argue his designation of her, rather, she asserted her own voice and need to be lifted up.

I had decided some time ago that when a white person asks me where I am from, I would reply, "from Vancouver." So at a check-out counter, when a tall, white male eyed me curiously and asked me where I was from, I was ready. But readiness is a David next to a Goliath of systemic racism. "But what is your nationality?" was his response after a predictable pause. "I'm Canadian." "Oh, I see," he answered wisely with an upward tilt of his head and a downward, dubious glance at me. I let the silence tell us both the story of the moment. Then he clung to his rightness and his privilege to ask, and to comment, "It's just that some of us are darker than others."

And so when Jesus said to the Syro-phoenician woman to "let the children (read, the privileged class) be fed first, for it is not fair to take the children's food and throw it to the dogs (read, those of other non-white races or non-Eurocentric cultures)," I know exactly the moment and the humiliation that pierces my heart. The courage to stay in the situation and speak my identity and truth is a moment of excruciating pain, and also of magnificent freedom.

Here is where the story ends for me. Assimilation and visibility no longer ease the pain of the heart. What is required is transformation as a concrete event in the hearts of those who have had a voice, decision-making power, and privilege within the institution. It is no longer acceptable for me to say, as the Syro-phoenician woman said, "Sir, even the dogs under the table eat the children's crumbs." To say this would be to collude and perpetuate a structure of racial and cultural dominance.

The Syro-phoenician woman teaches us to be confident and self-respecting, believing that we deserve to be seen, heard, make decisions, and lead because *I am*. She teaches us to say, "You are mistaken. These are not dogs. These are children who need to sit at a table and eat as the other children already at the table eat. No one will eat the crumbs, Sir. We will all partake of the banquet for there is enough for everyone. Sir, your humble transformation is an inspiration to us all. Go. May your ministry continue to be graced by transformations such as this."

Reflection

Read the story of the Syro-phoenician woman again. Hear this story *not* from Jesus' point of view but from the perspective of the ethnic woman (this is the fresh view).

Find a prayer, song, or poem by a racial-ethnic minority person. Place it in your place of prayer. Meditate on this.

What insights and grace are you receiving?

If you had difficulty or were unable to find writings by someone from a non-dominant race or culture, what does this say to you?

PRAYER

[This is the "Our Father and Mother" in Pilipino, formerly known as Tagalog. It can be read phonetically as is. Say it aloud to yourself and experience the movement of transformation in this symbolic act.]

Ama at ina namin, sumasalangit
ka
sambahin ang ngalan mo
Mapasaamin ang kaharian mo,
sundin and loob mo
Dito sa lupa para nang sa langit.
Bigyan mo kami ngayon ng amin
kakanin sa araw-araw
At patawarin mo kami sa aming
mga sala
Para ng pagpapatawad namin sa
nagkakasala sa amin
At huwag mo kaming
ipahintulot sa tukso
At iadya mo kami sa lahat ng
masama.

Thursday

BROKEN PROMISES

Karyn Bigby

EXODUS 7:25-8:19

"But when Pharaoh saw that there was a respite (from the plague of the frogs), he hardened his heart, and would not listen to them, just as the Lord had said."

Pharaoh's many broken promises to Moses reminds me of the story of the parishioner who told his minister if he ever had the money, he would love to contribute more to the church. One day, the parishioner inherited a large sum of money. When the minister called on him to fulfil his promise, the parishioner replied, "When I had the mind, I didn't have the money. Now that I have the money, I don't have the mind."

We often break the promises we make in church. We join when times are rough and as our situation gets better, we fail to remember our promises to God. Or we join when things are going well and when things go wrong, we are angry at God. At baptism, we promise to bring up our children in the church, yet we break that promise. We make vows to our spouse at the time of our marriage, yet we break those promises as well.

Like Pharaoh, "plagues" sometimes

befall us when we break our promises to God. Our children suffer when they grow up without knowledge of the love of God. Suffering and mistrust are often the result of marital breakdown.

God promised us that he would become one of us through his son, Jesus Christ. God kept his promise. God also promises that if we believe, we will experience everlasting life: "...in accordance with God's promise, we wait for new heavens and a new earth, where righteousness is at home." (2 Peter 3:13)

According to the Basis of Union, a primary tenet of The United Church of Canada is to foster the spirit of unity. The motto of the United Church, ut omnes unum sint ("that all may be one") is confirmation that The United Church of Canada is to be a united and uniting church. One would expect that this unity not only related to denominational components but to all its people, irrespective of racial or cultural background. Unfortunately, this is not the reality for segments of the church membership. We must try to be sensitive to others if we are to be truly united and uniting.

What cultural images are presented in your worship service? Can you identify with these images? Do you find your church a community in which you feel accepted? I cringe at some of the language and imagery used. Why is good always depicted as white, and sin and evil black? Does this mean that I am an evil person because I am Black?

Reflection

How can we keep our promises to God?

How can we help each other keep our promises together?

Prayer

Lord, you never let us down.
You never break your promises
to us.
Help us keep our promises to
you
and to remember that you
sacrificed
your son, Jesus Christ,
for our sakes.

Friday

GIVING UP ARROGANCE

Nena Cervantes

2 CORINTHIANS 4:13-18

"...Because we look not at what can be seen but at what cannot be seen; for what can be seen is temporary, but what cannot be seen is eternal."

I had read about the Rift Valley before driving to it from Nairobi, Kenya. Still, no description ever matched seeing it. I tried to capture its magnificence through a camera, but shots from different angles would not suffice. I could not capture either its breadth and depth or convey its atmosphere of timelessness. To have a sense of its grandeur requires a plane ride over Kenya, Tanzania, and Uganda. Scientists attribute this massive indentation on the earth's surface to volcanic shifts which occurred in this part of East Africa eons ago, or to a meteor. What struck me was the unseen power propelling a meteor earthbound like a giant shotput.

Lent may be, for some, a time for giving up something. When my memories revisit the Rift Valley, I give up the arrogant concept that I, as a human being, stand at the apex of the animal kingdom, that Mother Earth lies supine for me to trample on.

REFLECTION

How do we stay in touch with the unseen when in the presence of natural beauty?

What arrogance can you give up?

PRAYER

Sublime Creator,
make us as wide and open as the valley
in the presence of those who are different,
for our gifts may vary
but our Donor is the same.

Saturday

IMAGINARY HOMELAND

Richard Chung-sik Choe

PSALM 137
"By the rivers of Babylon—there we sat and wept, when we remembered Zion....How could we sing the Lord's song in a foreign land?"

One of the worst feelings I experienced as a child was waking up from a nap and finding myself alone. It was late afternoon in South Korea and my mother had gone shopping for dinner preparation. My brothers were playing with their friends outside. I called for my mother as I slowly awakened. No one was home.

I am in my mid-thirties now and I have a family of my own. Both my parents and my brothers live within a half hour driving distance. But sometimes I still wake up at night feeling so utterly alone, so abandoned. It is an experience of such vast emptiness that, while that feeling lasts, I know that absolutely nothing will be able to fill that void. A torrent of "memory-rush" sweeps in and takes me way beyond my childhood—all the way to time immemorial it seems. It is a surge of pain and emptiness from such depths of my being that I just want to collapse and wail and ail and lament at life so barren and empty. And I begin to understand what it means to feel like a motherless child.

I name it "in-transit" feeling, a feeling that originates from being "in-between." I have lived in Canada for more than 20 years—more than half my lifetime. And yet, no matter how many years I live here, no matter how many friends and acquaintances I have made, I cannot help feeling that I will always be regarded as a stranger in this land.

Growing up in Canada as a visible minority immigrant is about learning to live with the existential pain of being "homeless" in your country; it is learning that the first immigrants treat the newer immigrants as a threat to their land. It is learning that you can never go back to what was once home because everything changes with time.

Being a visible minority in Canada is to be eternally condemned for the odyssey to the imaginary homeland. Disconnected from the past and yet bound by it. It is a longing so powerful, fuelled by a sense of loss and an urge to reclaim the past, that one wants to leave everything and run. But where to? Where is the "homeland" I am searching for?

Like the Israelites of the Babylonian exile, I long for the home where everyone can find love and remembrance of belonging. However, unlike the exiles who desperately desired to return to their homeland, I dream of journeying into the heartland of Canada, and finding my "imaginary homeland." A place where people's lives and futures are bound together in love. I dream of Canada as a place where refugees and immigrants of old and new dare to hope for the future together with the peoples of the First Nations.

We are all on a journey through this "in-transit" experience bringing both hope and fear in us. A journey into the future with a dream that each of us is a vessel that carries the memories of our God and ancestors who are one. Through this "in-transit" journey, I fiercely search for God to lead me to the imaginary homeland.

REFLECTION

What stereotypes come to mind when you hear the words Black, white, yellow, red, men, women, Anglophone, Francophone, gay, lesbian, new immigrants, refugees?

What is home to them?

What kind of home would your church community be for them?

How would you be able to live with them as brothers or sisters in your world?

PRAYER

God of our ancestors,
disconnected from your love,
we are like motherless children;
separated from one another,
abandoned by one another.
We are like the "homeless,"
distanced from one group or tribe
to another.
Bring us home so that we can
experience what it means to be
a family with you as our Mother
and Father,
to be a brother or a sister to one
another,
to share earth as a common
shelter, a home,
with those who call one another
friends in your love,
and those who treasure one
another as your gift to us.

Part Seven - Coming Home

Palm/Passion Sunday

CELEBRATE A NEW WORLD ORDER

Eleanor Scarlett

ZECHARIAH 9: 9-12

"Rejoice greatly, O daughter Zion! Shout aloud, O daughter Jerusalem! Lo, your king comes to you; triumphant and victorious is he, humble and riding on a donkey, on a colt, the foal of a donkey."

As a displaced African living in the West, I remember hearing my people tell stories of liberation, stories called Caribbean folklore. Older members of these communities will argue that these tales originated in Africa.

"It is dark and the people are suffering. There is gloom everywhere; hopelessness and helplessness have become the theme of the day. The International Monetary Fund has withdrawn its support. Multi-national corporations have replaced the old system. Crime has increased and people are afraid to leave their homes. The familiar cry is one of hunger, pain, and anguish. These have replaced the slave master's whip.

"There is singing in the distance; it appears to be a celebration. How can they celebrate when there is so much hardship? Mother Pinnock has a vision: God's promise is soon to be fulfilled in the birth of a Saviour. In the vision, she saw Ayesha pregnant. It is her baby who will be the One. How can this be? She is only a poor 16-year old single girl from the village. No one will ever believe Mother Pinnock; this time she has gone too far. The people listened and have pondered in their hearts, and remembered that prophets of old told them that the Saviour would be born from a humble African home. So maybe it is true; they have suffered long and hard, and it is time for some celebration. They could find no hope in politicians. God, the source of their hope, did not forget their plight, but kept the promise that was made with their ancestors a long time ago to send us a liberator who would save them from these difficulties."

This is a wonderful message that I will never forget. Displaced Africans of the world have often asked, "How long, Lord, how long?" Suffering continues today in the form of economic hardships and oppression.

North America has not yet addressed the plight of those of us who are here. Some of us came because of economic reasons and the need for a better life. Others have been here for centuries. Some of us are just finding out who we really are as a people. It is here that we are striving to achieve real change, not only on a spiritual level, but also economically. As a people, unless we can achieve economic self-determination, we will never be able to find our rightful place in this world order, or the one to come. The ripple effect of our displacement still haunts our survival.

Despite our despair, there is hope in knowing that we as a people can still see stars at night.

The Messiah will come to liberate us from our struggles. The Messiah will bring about changes to the hearts of all peoples. The Messiah will come as a humble, lowly human being with no fanfare, no Rolls Royce, and no rolled out carpet, but riding on a donkey. The new world order will be one of peace and harmony, where all God's children will dwell together within this household of freedom. Then true celebration will begin.

REFLECTION

What can we do to make a difference?

How can we begin a ripple effect of celebration?

PRAYER

Spirit of God,
we give you thanks for the gift of
your son Jesus the Christ,
who was born as an ordinary
man.
He came to bring about world
equality and peace.
Help us to acknowledge that
even though
we are sojourners in this world,
You have given us the
knowledge of faith
that will lead us to a deeper
understanding of your love
for us.

Monday

Remember Silent Stories

Kim Uyede-Kai

Lamentations 1:1-2, 6-12
"Jerusalem remembers, in the days of her affliction and wandering, all the precious things that were hers in days of old."

My mother's mother,
my grandmother,
crippled by a stroke
when her eldest daughter
was fifteen
crippling her youth,
silencing the stories.

Stories
of a Japanese woman
married to a man she did not know
a man born in Canada
a man whose culture was her own
yet not.

Stories
of a hard life in an unknown land
a Japanese woman
isolated by language
from English neighbours
isolated by sea
from Japanese family.

Not silent then
(did she laugh?)
raising four children
her voice living on
through them
"thread for your needle
no longer than to your elbow"
"eat every grain of rice
or you will go blind."

But no stories of war
called dirty jap
enemy alien
losing the things that were home
silent pain
silent suffering.

Bedridden
silent presence
silent stories
light the Buddhist incense
at the cemetery
at the home altar.

Voiceless stories
silently scenting
the childhood of
her granddaughter
me.

Reflection

Perhaps using an old photo album, remember a time of celebration, high spirits, good feeling.

Talk about what was precious about that remembrance.

Hold in your mind a memory of aching and wandering.

Gently, tenderly, silently embrace it with acceptance, comfort, forgiveness.

Release the memory with care. Dwell in the silence.

Prayer

Comforting God of our
grandmothers and our
mothers,
of our grandfathers and our
fathers,
We rely so heavily on words,
the spoken word,
the written word,
to bind us together
to the days of old.

Where are you in the
wordlessness
of our lives?
Where are you in the stillness
between the words?
Could it be that we only listen
when we want to hear words?
Could it be that we are listening
with expectations of how we will
hear
instead of just listening?

In times of remembering
what was precious,
in times of affliction and
wandering,
Teach us to allow you to
turn wordless silences
into pulsing sounds
of the heart.

Tuesday

MINISTRY TO ALL PEOPLE

Alex Kasirye-Musoke

2 CORINTHIANS 1:8-24
"...We are workers with you for your joy, because you stand firm in the faith."

Paul tells the church at Corinth that it is God who called them together to share in Christ's life and suffering. He also calls them to rely, not on themselves, but on God in Christ. This, for Paul, means being fully involved with all people just like Christ was. He warns the church against deception and evasiveness. He encourages the church to be straightforward, understanding, and caring in its approach to people, to foster mutual confidence and respect, gifts from God.

Paul's letter still has much to say to today's church in its treatment of its clergy as well as its laity. Coming from Uganda to Canada, I sought to minister to Anglican parishes. I was told that what I really should do was go back to Uganda because the church there could use me more. Was I not wanted in ministry here because I was from Uganda? Could a Ugandan born minister not be needed to minister to Canadians? I did, in fact, minister to two parishes, but eventually transferred to the United Church.

Paul's view is that each member has been called to be a minister to all people and tells them that the call to being a minister has many things that go with it. It is a call to keeping one's eyes and ears open to the voice of God through all people. It is a call to a personal relationship with Jesus Christ and to integrity for the benefit of the entire community. It means seeing beyond the limitations we have put on the roles of clergy and laity, and on culture, race, and country of origin.

Like Paul, we call on the church to proclaim the gospel of Christ with sincerity and a positive attitude. It is also a call to us to ask what it means to minister to all people.

REFLECTION
How do you compare your local church with the church of Corinth?

How can we hear the voice of God in all people?

PRAYER

Almighty God,
Help us to understand what
your will is
in the confusion and unrest of
our times.
Teach us to listen and hear you
speak.
Let your will be done in your
holy church.

Wednesday

Doing God's Will

Karyn Bigby

Mark 12:1-11

"The stone that the builders rejected has become the cornerstone."

Dr. Martin Luther King, Jr. is one of my heroes. I admire him for his commitment to non-violence, his belief that we are all God's children, his strong commitment to the Civil Rights Movement, and to ending the segregation of Blacks and whites. But mostly I admire him because he spoke about being judged by the content of our characters, not by the colour of our skin, an issue with which I, too, must deal with on a daily basis.

Just as Jesus, rejected by the religious leaders of his day, predicted his death in the parable of the wicked tenants, so too did Dr. King. On Saturday, February 4, 1968, he told the people of Ebenezer Baptist Church in Atlanta, Georgia:

> Every now and then I think about my own death, and I think about my own funeral. I don't think about it in a morbid sense. Every now and then I ask myself, "What is it that I want said?" And I leave the word to you this morning. If any of you are around when I have to meet my day, I don't want a long funeral. And if you get somebody to deliver the eulogy, tell them not to talk too long. Tell them not to mention that I have a Nobel Peace Prize. That isn't important. Tell them not to mention that I have three or four hundred other awards. That's not important.
>
> I'd like somebody to mention that day that Martin Luther King, Jr. tried to love somebody. I want you to be able to say that day that I did try to feed the hungry. I want you to be able to say that I did try in my life to clothe those who were naked....I want you to say that I tried to love and serve humanity....And all of the other shallow things will not matter. I won't have the fine and luxurious things of life to leave behind. I just want to leave a committed life behind...." [15]

On Wednesday, April 3, 1968, the evening before he was assassinated, Dr. King again addressed the issue of his forthcoming death:

> We've got some difficult days ahead. But it really doesn't matter with me now. Because I've been to the mountaintop. Like anybody, I would like to live a long life. Longevity has its place. But I'm not concerned about that now. I just

want to do God's will. And [God's] allowed me to go up to the mountain. And I've looked over, and I've seen the Promised Land. I may not get there with you, but I want you to know tonight that we as a people will get to the Promised Land. So, I'm happy tonight. I'm not fearing any man. Mine eyes have seen the glory of the coming of the Lord." [16]

During his funeral at Ebenezer Baptist Church, a tape of his February 4 address was played. In essence, Dr. King delivered his own eulogy.

REFLECTION

How do you live out God's purpose in your daily life?

What do you think people will see as your legacy?

PRAYER

Loving God,
We thank you for the lives of
those prophets
who so faithfully lived out your
purpose for them,
and who worked so hard for the
rights of others:
for survival, for education, for
freedom, and dignity.
Grant that their legacies may live
on in our lives.

Maundy Thursday

ONE BREAD, ONE BODY

Nena Cervantes

I CORINTHIANS 10:14-17

"Because there is one bread, we who are many are one body, for we all partake of the one bread."

In 1990, my family held a reunion in Manila. We, as a nuclear family, had not seen one another since our parents' demise over 10 years ago. We flew in from Canada, Germany, and the U.S. to be together for a month. When our nuclear family gathered together with the extended family, we ranged from an 80-year old aunt who was a minister, to a six-year old nephew who was a reformed "Dennis the Menace." English, Spanish, German, Tagalog, Ilonggo, and Cebuano languages and dialects were spoken.

The more things had changed, the more they remained the same. My German brother-in-law still scratched his head when salt was put on pineapples, and stayed a safe distance while his daughter took lessons from her Filipino-Spanish cousin on how to select and eat good durian, a delicious fruit with a potent odour. My Spanish brother-in-law, who had come to the Philippines as a child, still held his nose to jackfruit, but loved all other tropical fruits. My Irish-American brother-in-law could not make it, but my sister flew in with their daughters.

On the stairwell towards the bedrooms in the home where we gathered hung a picture a nephew had bought in Paris. It was the torso of a Christ-like figure appearing to rise up. The song by John B. Foley, "One Bread, One Body" came to mind as I looked down to the living room and dining room where people who could have been enemies during two past world wars were now kith and kin, supping together, singing together, worshipping together, partaking of that one bread.

REFLECTION

How did early Christians live together to create a loving, caring community?

In what ways can we extend our sense of family to a global level?

How can we eat and drink worthily together as a global family?

PRAYER

Loving God,
Our world is becoming a global village.
May we live as early Christians did:
spreading the words of hope and love.
Living those words through our daily deeds.

Good Friday

CRYING FOR A DREAM

Richard Chung-sik Choe

JOHN 19:38-42

"(After the crucifixion of Jesus) Joseph of Arimathea...(and) Nicodemus ...took the body of Jesus...to a tomb nearby...(and) laid Jesus there."

The death of Jesus. Night fell silently, tenderly as his followers carried the marred and broken body of their teacher. With death descended sorrow and fear in the hearts of the followers of the Way of Jesus of Nazareth, the Way abruptly ended at Golgotha, the Place of the Skull. No more life, no more hope—just shattered dreams of what might have been the way to God's Reign. Where to go from here? How to find a way out?

I have always associated Good Friday with broken dreams: of Jesus, his followers, and God. Recently, a passage from Mary Crow Dog's book *Lakota Woman* helped me to understand more about the meaning of the death and entombment of Jesus.

Crying for a dream ("hanbeleceya") is what the Lakota people call it. When the community can no longer find its way out, such is a time for a vision quest. The medicine man or woman goes into the earth womb to seek a clear vision for the community. Mary

Crow Dog speaks of her experience of crying for a dream in this way:

> In a way the vision seeker is dead while crying for a dream....A vision quest lasts for four days and nights. Inside the pit you lose all sensations of having a body....You feel nothing, see nothing, hear nothing, taste nothing, because during a "hanbeleceya" you do not eat or drink. It is scary to cry for a dream, to be entirely thrown upon yourself, not knowing whether you are awake, asleep, or even alive....[17]

As I try to imagine the body of Jesus lying in a dark tomb near Gethsemane, I imagine the gentle and tender night enveloping Jesus. In that darkness Jesus dreams of a world where humanity and creation can be one with each other and with God, a world where pain and death is but a sign of hope and healing. Even violent death on the cross cannot crush God's dream to have mutual relations with God's creation. Jesus died on the way to bringing this Good News to the world.

We believe in God who dares to dream to be one with us. God's dream continues when we feed the hungry, when we embrace those who have been labelled as less than others, when we comfort those who are grieving through the loss of loved ones. To dream for one another is our ministry with Jesus Christ today. That is how we find our way out to the world where shattered dreams can be healed and made whole again.

Good Friday is about more than dying. For we who believe, it is about dreaming. It is about participating in God's dream of healing the world, God's creation. It is about being whole again.

Reflection

What broken dreams are to be mended for you?

What would help you to start on that journey of healing and to be dreaming once again?

How would you be able to dream with others as a faith community?

Prayer

God of Dream,
I search for you in darkness
to find you and to dream with
you once again.
I remember the pain of being
different,
I remember how I learned to
clench my fists
as I struggled so hard to be
accepted,

I remember those nights,
desperately searching for
you to comfort me.
God of Dream,
now I know that you are the
tears of my pain,
you are the broken hearts of
those who suffer in this
world,
you are the night that comes
tenderly to heal and to
dream
with those who are searching for
your Way.
Guide me as I learn to dream
with you.
Walk with me as I learn to open
my arms to embrace those in
need
and to wipe away tears with
those who are crying for
your dreams to come true.

Holy Saturday

EXAMINE OUR WAYS

Alex Kasirye-Musoke

LAMENTATIONS 3:37-58

"Let us test and examine our ways, and return to the Lord; let us lift up our hearts, as well as our hands, to God in heaven."

We know the way. We know where we should be or what we should be doing. The writer calls us to examine our ways to find out whether we are on the right track in our behaviour, outlook, actions, and response to both God and our neighbours. It also refers to our response to the Ten Commandments or the shamah, "Love the Lord your God with all your heart, and with all your soul, and with all your mind, and with all your strength, and your neighbour as you love yourself."

We are reminded to ask ourselves questions like, "Have I kept God in the centre of my life? Have I surrendered fully to the command and will of God? Can I confidently say, 'I am fully thine, Lord'?"

Loving God is no simple matter. There are things we need to do and not do. That is why when we repent of our sins we say, "Lord forgive us those things we have done when we were not expected to do them, things we have not done when we were expected to do them; and things we have said when we were not expected to say them and things we have not said when we were expected to say them." We need to check ourselves constantly to see whether we are still doing God's will.

In his teaching Jesus said, "If you love me, carry your cross and follow me." Christ carried his own cross and gave us each our own cross to carry. Some of our crosses are capable of turning us away from God: a chronic illness, a relationship, money problems, death of someone we love, or anything that weighs us down. When we examine ourselves, we can see how powerless and weak we are. We also become aware of Christ's presence with us and his ability to help us carry our cross. This means putting Christ ahead of us and all that we do. In other words, getting our priorities right.

"Let us lift our hearts (first) not our hands, to God in heaven." Let us come before the throne of God, bringing the centre of our lives, the heart, to God. The heart is the centre of our being and operation. It is what we have to offer to God first if anything else is to follow.

When we lift our hearts as a token of our love, God fills them with love, the love we share with others through the labours of our hands. So when we lift our hearts we are also keeping our hands and our feet ready to serve both God and humanity. Today is the day to examine ourselves. May God help us.

REFLECTION

What do you regard as your cross?

How easily do you share this burden with friends, family or with God?

How has sharing it with others helped in any way?

PRAYER

Merciful God,
thank you for being there for me
    in times of temptation.
I lift before you all those who
    doubt your love,
pray for those who find it
    difficult to believe or to
    pray;
and for those who have not
    found hope or lost hope in
    you.
May your light shine upon and
    lead them
into the paths of
truth and righteousness.
In Jesus Christ's name I pray.

Easter Sunday

CHAOS AND CREATION

Marilou Carrillo

ISAIAH 51:9-11
"Awake, awake, put on strength, O arm of the Lord!"

I stood in the rain one evening in a circle of Filipino women and others in solidarity, mourning the death of a domestic worker hanged in Singapore. I felt both rage and power. The prayers, the stories, the systemic analysis from speakers reflected the chaos of evil and despair as well as the creation of community and action. We shouted our anger and the rage of God at grave injustice and the taking of a life. We spoke out against the systems of dominance that led to such a death.

The Philippine government exporting migrant workers is a billion dollar industry. The Singaporean government extracts levies for each worker and offers no protection. This bilateral agreement is a showcase of modern slavery. We declared the ongoing struggle to defend the rights of domestic workers and other migrant workers all over the world, where the wealthy utilize and pay for them. We lamented, wept, and acted.

"Awake, awake! Clothe yourself in strength, arm of Yahweh." Why the silence when here we stand weeping for a sister-slave? Yes, you say you played a part in bringing the Israelites from slavery to freedom, through the "waters of the great Abyss." How will our sisters and brothers be brought out of slavery as domestic workers in the homes of the wealthy and powerful, in sweatshops and factories, away from their own children? You promised that those who were scattered will return. When will this happen for those who sit in loneliness, isolation, poverty, and physical and sexual abuse from Scotland to Saudi Arabia? When will they return to their homeland?

You say "they will enter Zion shouting for joy, their heads crowned with joy unending; joy and gladness will escort them and sorrow and sighing will take flight." We want to believe you, your words, and your faithfulness. We lit candles in that circle. We looked at each other's eyes. We spoke and heard each other's voices. We believed in ourselves and our sisters and brothers throughout the globe. We believed in life and the future. We sang a song of the land of our birth.

And then we all went home. Isaiah forgot to mention this part: that for our people's freedom, it will be a very long, hard, joyful, victorious tomorrow.

REFLECTION

Think of a Two-Thirds World immigrant, refugee, or Canadian-born racial-ethnic person you know. Name her/him. Think of his/her story. On a piece of paper, draw what you know about her/his journey. (If you don't know, ask next time you see this person.) Place this in front of you as you meditate on the suffering of his/her entire community.

Who is in solidarity with these persons or their community? Who are exploiting them? Who are the onlookers?

How do you/we in our communities lament this injustice?

Who has the power to move from chaos to creation, from slavery to freedom?

PRAYER

O Author of Myth and History
Hear the cry of the poor.
You who cry out against
injustice
Hear our shouts of rage and
indignation
for all who die and suffer at the
hands
of those who believe in greed,
death, and destruction.
You who weep when one of us
suffers and dies
Listen to those who work in
hard labour,
away from their children and
their homeland.
You who suffer your own death
at the lost lives of the poor,
Walk with us throughout the
earth
where workers sit in loneliness
and despair.

O Risen Spirit
Who walked with us and taught
us
to create new life in the midst of
chaos
Who awakened our spirits and
our lives from slavery to
freedom
Be with us now and in the future
to struggle and stand in your
power
Until we have all come home in
joy and gladness.

Endnotes

1. Micklem, Caryl ed. *More Contemporary Prayers: Prayers on Fifty-two Themes.* (London: SCM Press Ltd.) 1970.

2. Ellison, Ralph *Invisible Man.* (New York: The Modern Library) 1992.

3. Kawano, Roland *The Global City.* (Winfield: Wood Lake Books, Inc.) 1992.

4. Hill, Daniel G. *The Freedom Seekers: Blacks in Early Canada.* (Agincourt: The Book Society of Canada) 1981, 26.

5. Ibid., 38.

6. Akers, Doris Copyright 1958 by MANNA MUSIC, 2111 Kenmere Ave., Burbank, CA 91504 USA. Copyright secured. All Rights Reserved.

7. Heyward, Carter "Living for the Living: Theological Lessons from Nicaragua," Davis, Ellen C., ed. *Speaking of Christ: A Lesbian Feminist Voice*. (New York: The Pilgrim Press) 1989.

8. hooks, bell *Outlaw Culture: Resisting Representation*. (New York: Routledge) 1994.

9. Park, Andrew Sung *The Wounded Heart of God: The Asian Concept of Han and the Christian Doctrine of Sin*. (Nashville: Abingdon Press) 1993.

10. Ibid.

11. Ibid.

12. Volavkova, Hana, ed. *...I Never Saw Another Butterfly...: Children's Drawings and Poems from Terezin Concentration Camp 1942-1944*. (New York: Schocken Books) 1993.

13. Ibid.

14. Maria del Nevo *The New Internationalist*, #240. February 1993, 22.

15. Oates, Stephen B. *Let the Trumpet Sound: The Life of Martin Luther King, Jr.* (New York: New American Library) 1982.

16. Bennett, Lerone Jr. *What Manner of Man: A Biography of Martin Luther King, Jr. 1929-1968.* (Chicago: Johnson Publishing Company Inc.) 1976.

17. Mary Crow Dog *Lakota Woman*. (Grove Weidenfeld) 1990.

About the Authors

Karyn Bigby was born in Kingston, Jamaica. Her family emigrated to Canada when she was four-years old and settled in southern Ontario before moving to Montreal. Karyn graduated from Queens University with a B.A. (Honours) in Economics and History, and an MBA, specializing in Marketing. She presently works in the field of Specialty Advertising. She is a member of Union United Church Gospel Choir and manages the choir's heavily booked appearance schedule. Karyn is married to David Edey, a financial planner, and they are expecting their first child.

Marilou Carrillo is a first generation Filippina Canadian whose interests include multicultural education, interfaith issues, human rights, and group processes. She holds degrees in both speech and language pathology, and theology. She has worked with health and rural groups in Merida, Venezuela and served on the Amnesty International (Canadian) Board. She is currently a speech language pathologist in Vancouver, and a group facilitator for social and religious groups. Marilou researched, wrote stories, and contributed liturgy to the resource *Tales of Interracial Marriage*. She was theological reflector for the Division of Mission in Canada and is a member of the Anti-Racism Task Group.

Nena Cervantes lived in Manila, New York, and Montreal prior to moving to Toronto. She has visited 22 countries in four continents where she has had opportunities to appreciate many cultures. She has been active in Bloor Street United Church local outreach committees as a member and recorder, and on a steering committee to minister to recent immigrants using alternative structures of pastoral care and worship. She took a course on doing ministry in a multicultural setting at the Centre for Christian Studies and has attended ecumenical church conferences on anti-racism, faith, and social justice issues. Nena was a planning team member of "Sounding the Bamboo II," a United Church conference for racial/ ethnic minority women.

Richard Chung-sik Choe has been working with Bethesda of Forest Glen United Church in Mississauga since 1989 as an ordained minister. He has also been deeply involved in dreaming, planning, and establishing the Ethnic Ministries Council of The United Church of Canada. Richard is South Korean born and came to Canada as a youth. He enjoys writing and leading workshops on cultural diversity and other social justice issues. Richard and his spouse, Sung, have two daughters, Frances and Michelle.

Alex Kasirye-Musoke was born in Uganda. He trained in Economics at Makerere University and was a teacher of economics and an economics consultant. He did theological training to become a lay minister at the University of Nottingham in England before becoming a political refugee. After a period of asylum in Kenya, he came to Canada where he obtained a Ph.D. in theology from the University of Toronto. He served as an Anglican minister to two parishes before transferring to the United Church in 1992. Alex is married to Elizabeth, and they have four children: Mikol, Tendo, Suubi, and Muyinza.

Eleanor Scarlett was born and raised into a Methodist family in Jamaica where her grandmothers were the nurturers of her earliest years. After a career as a nurse in psychiatric care both in Jamaica and in Canada, she began working on her Master of Divinity degree at the Toronto School of Theology, Emmanuel College. Eleanor did her internship in Nova Scotia and is completing her studies. She is looking forward to ordered ministry in The United Church of Canada.

Kim Uyede-Kai is a fourth generation Japanese Canadian and has a keen interest in cultural diversity issues. She has been involved with the feasibility task group and implementation group for the Ethnic Ministries Council of the United Church. She has also been involved as a volunteer with various church courts and committees, and is a third generation United Church member. She has a B.A.A. in Social Services and is an occasional freelance writer. She recently began theological studies in the Master of Divinity programme at Emmanuel College. Kim and her husband, Brian Kai, live in Etobicoke and are parents of Trevor and Jeremy.